BOOK 2

A STUDENT'S GUIDE AND WORKBOOK
ENGLISH GRAMMAR

John Lee

STONE TOWER PRESS

A Student's Guide and
Workbook to English Grammar
Book 2

Stone Tower Press
7 Ellen Rd.
Middletown, RI 02842
stonetowerpress.com

Paperback ISBN: 978-1-7368651-4-9

Formatting and cover design by Amy Cole, JPL Design Solutions

About the Cover Image:
The classical owl tetradrachm is the most recognized coin of the ancient world. In Greek mythology the owl accompanied Athena, the goddess of wisdom. The owl, in time, became a symbol of knowledge, wisdom, and learning—a veritable mascot for education.

Printed in the United States of America

Revised edition

TABLE OF CONTENTS

Diagnostic Test 7

I. Parts of Speech 11

1. Verbs 13
2. Nouns 17
3. Adjectives 19
4. Pronouns 22
5. Adverbs 25
6. Prepositions 28
7. Conjunctions 31
8. Interjections 33

Parts of Speech Test: 34

II. Parts of the Sentence 41

9. The Predicate 43
10. The Subject 45
11. Direct Objects 48
12. Indirect Objects 50
13. Prepositional Phrases 52
14. Appositives 55

Parts of the Sentence Test: 56

III. Clauses 61

15. Clauses 63
16. Noun Clauses 72
17. Who and Whom 79
18. Types of Sentences 84

Clause Test: 90

IV. Verbals 95
19. Gerunds 97
20. Participles I 105
21. Participles II 112
Clauses and Participles: 126
22. Infinitives I 131
23. Infinitives II 138
Verbal Practice: 142
Verbal and Clause Practice: 145
Verbal Test: 150
About the Author 156

TO STUDENTS

This volume is a continuation of book 1 where the parts of speech, the parts of a sentence, and clauses were examined. It builds on and assumes knowledge of these topics. That said, because review is a cardinal part of learning, this book starts with a review of book 1, along with a diagnostic assessment and three unit tests before moving onto the heart of this book—verbals.

Students can find verbals difficult because they are an amalgam of various parts of speech. Gerunds are verbal nouns, participles are verbal adjectives, and infinitives are words that function as adjectives, adverbs, and nouns. Knowing that verbals can be tricky, I have added extra exercises, especially in the section that deals with participles and infinitives. There is also a section on dangling participles, which, I hope, amuses students and clarifies their thinking.

Also, like the first book, the additional exercises present more difficult sentences. If students can do them, they can be sure that they understand the concept. However, students should remember to proceed carefully. With the completion of this book, they will have covered all the rudiments of English grammar, an important milestone in the life of a student. Moreover, what they learn here will be with them for a lifetime, which is a remarkable accomplishment.

As I wrote in the introduction of book 1, students should not hesitate to ask their teachers clarifying questions in class. Learning material during class is the mark of maturity. Applying this lesson will save hours, not to mention frustration. I should also note that sections 1-16 have been slightly expanded—mostly additional examples. Finally, I've adding readings from various genres—philosophy, theology, commencements speeches, and more. Apart from dissecting these passages, take time to reflect on them. They are intended to provoke discussion and reflection.

Godspeed to all who move deeper in the study of grammar.

ACKNOWLEDGMENTS

A word of thanks goes to Tim Demy for his encouragement, expertise, and eye for detail. Without him, none of this would be possible. I also thank Amy Cole, whose artistic sense makes everything far more appealing and easier to use. A special thanks goes to Christina Mitchell whose comments on infinitives made that section much clearer and Josh Wilson whose feedback over the years has refined this volume. I also thank my former students, too many to name, for all their questions, good humor, and insights. Finally, I dedicate this book to my colleagues at the Geneva School of Manhattan. What a year! We have grown older and grayer (at least I have) but also wiser and more discerning. Solon's words have proved to be true. *γηράσκω δ' αἰεὶ πολλὰ διδασκόμενος*. For this point, I am grateful and look forward to many years of working and collaborating together in this high calling of education.

DIAGNOSTIC TEST

I. Identify the underlined words. Give the part of speech if applicable.

"The deep green pool **of the Salinas River** was still in the late afternoon. Already the sun had left the valley to go climbing up the slopes of the Gabilan Mountains,[1] and the hilltops were **rosy** in the sun. But by the pool among the mottled sycamores, a pleasant **shade** had fallen.

A water snake glided smoothly **up** the pool, twisting its periscope head from side to side; and it swam the **length** of the pool and came to the **legs** of a motionless heron that stood in the shallows. A silent head and beak lanced down and plucked it out by the head, and the beak swallowed the little snake **while its tail waved frantically**.

A far rush of wind sounded and a gust drove through the tops of the trees like a wave. The sycamore leaves turned up their silver sides, the brown, dry leaves on the ground scudded a few feet. And row on row of tiny wind waves flowed up the pool's green surface.

As quickly as it had come, the wind died, and the clearing was quiet **again**. The heron stood in the shallows, motionless and waiting. Another little water snake swam up the pool, turning its periscope head from side to side.

---

1 A mountain range in southern inner California.

Suddenly Lennie appeared out of the brush, and he came as silently as a creeping bear moves. The heron pounded the **air** with its wings, jacked itself clear of the water and flew off down river. The little snake slid in among the reeds at the **pool's** side.

Lennie came quietly to the pool's edge. He knelt down and drank, barely touching his lips to the water. When a little bird skittered **over** the dry leaves behind him, his head jerked up and he strained toward the sound with eyes and ears **until he saw the bird**, and then he dropped his head and drank again.

When he was finished, he sat **down** on the bank, with his side to the pool, **so that he could watch the trail's entrance**. He embraced his knees and laid his chin down on his knees.

The light climbed on out of the valley, and as it went, the tops of the mountains seemed to blaze with increasing brightness."

John Steinbeck, *Of Mice and Men*

II. Draw parentheses around dependent clauses and identify the type of clause: adjectival, adverbial, or nominal.

1. After the storm, we assessed how much damage was done to the structures.
2. The book on the table I love, but the book on the desk is average.
3. Whenever I smell the sea, I remember the time I spent in the Outer Banks with my family.

4. There are many coffee shops that have excellent coffee, but only one provides excellent service.

5. "There is nothing like looking if you want to find something. You certainly usually find something, if you look, but it is not always quite the something you were after." J. R. R. Tolkien, *The Hobbit*

6. "As Gregor Samsa awoke one morning from uneasy dreams, he found himself transformed in his bed into an enormous insect." Franz Kafka, *Metamorphosis*

7. "All we have to decide is what to do with the time that is given us." J. R. R. Tolkien, *Fellowship of the Ring*

8. "What we need more than ever is wisdom to know what we should do in the face of uncertainty," said the professor.

9. While we don't know how this transformation took place, the prologue of the play gives one clue.

10. My advice to you is what I heard as a child: never do tomorrow what you can do today.

11. Two pregnant mothers with children in carriages maneuver down the street, and a doorman finishing his shift insists on opening the door for them as they are about to cross the threshold of a local café.

12. She knows that time is limited, so she wants to make the most of it.

13. "There are some things you learn best in calm, and some in storm." Willa Cather, *The Song of the Lark*

14. The works that have passed the test of time have done so for good reason; they speak to the perennial issues of the human heart and predicament.

15. The goal of stories invites people to step into a narrative and to develop a sense of the world that can produce virtues.

16. "It is only with the heart that one can see rightly; what is essential is invisible to the eye." Antoine de Saint-Exupéry, *The Little Prince*

17. "It was the best of times, it was the worst of times, it was the age of wisdom, it was the age of foolishness, it was the epoch of belief, it was the epoch of incredulity, it was the season of Light, it was the season of Darkness, it was the spring of hope, it was the winter of despair." Charles Dickens, *A Tale of Two Cities*

18. "Don't ever tell anybody anything. If you do, you start missing everybody." J. D. Salinger, *The Catcher in the Rye*

19. In one famous story when Alexander the Great approached Diogenes and asked him if he wanted anything, Diogenes looked at him with contempt and asked him to "move a little out of my sun."

20. "Love is holy because it is like grace—the worthiness of its object is never really what matters." Marilynne Robinson, *Gilead*

ONE
PARTS OF SPEECH

1. VERBS

1.1 The heart of a sentence is the verb. There are two types of verbs: action and linking.

- Action verbs perform an action.
- Linking verbs do not perform an action. Instead, they connect the subject to what comes after the verb. Think of a linking verb as showing what someone or something is. Examples will make this point clear.

1.2 Action verbs:

- The boy **jumped** over the fence.
- I **hit** the ball.
- **Sit** down!
- Martin **scored** three points in the final seconds.

1.3 Linking verbs:

- My mother **is** a doctor.
- The teacher **will be** pleased.
- The cookies **are** good.
- She **became** a lawyer.
- He **will become** a great writer.
- We **were** friends.

Notice the linking verb shows what someone or something is.

1.4 Tricky linking verbs:

- Apart from the verbs "to be" and "become," there are other linking verbs. Additional linking verbs include: *look, prove, smell, sound, taste, appear, and feel.*

To test whether a verb is a linking verb, replace the word with the appropriate form of the verb "to be." If the sentence makes sense, then the verb is a linking verb.

- The cake smells good. = The cake is good.
- She looks elated. = She is elated.
- That pasta tastes amazing. = That pasta is amazing.
- My mother appears satisfied. = My mother is satisfied.
- My friend smelled the roses. ≠ My friend is the roses.
- I looked at the dog. ≠ I am at the dog.
- John tasted the pasta. ≠ John is the pasta.
- My mother felt the kitten. ≠ My mother is the kitten.

1.5 Verbs can include more than one word. When this happens, all the words constitute a verb phrase. The words in the phrase are called helping or auxiliary verbs.

- I **am enjoying** the ice cream.
- I **should be enjoying** the ice cream.
- **Will** I **enjoy** the ice cream? (Notice the verb phrase is broken up by the subject.)
- I **will have been** president by then.
- I **had had** some of the cake. (Don't be fooled by the verb "had" and the auxiliary word "had.")
- She **might be coming** to the party.
- Recognizing verb phrases will help tremendously in Latin composition.

- The farmer is laboring. ~~*Agricola est laborat*~~. *Agricola laborat.*

1.6 Verbs are either passive or active in voice.

- The soldiers defended the city. (Active, the subject does the action.)
- The city was defended by the soldiers. (Passive, the subject receives the action.)
- The girl walked the dog. (Active)
- The dog was walked by the girl. (Passive)

1.7 Negative adverbs are not a part of the verb phrase.

- I **am** not your father, Luke. (Notice that the word, "not" is not in bold.)
- **Will** I not **give** you money? (Helping verbs do not need to be next to the main verb.)
- I **would**n't do that if I **were** you.
- Why **should** I not **spend** my money?

1.8 Action verbs can be either transitive or intransitive. Transitive verbs can take direct objects and intransitive verbs cannot. Some verbs are both transitive and intransitive. Context determines the nature of the verb.

- She **bumped** the boy. (Transitive)
- She **hit** the ball with the bat. (Transitive)
- She **walks** in the park. (Intransitive)
- She **walks** the dog in the park. (Transitive)
- She **stands**. (Intransitive)
- She **stands** the book on the table. (Transitive)

1.9 Verbs have three principal parts: Present tense, past tense, and past participle.

- Regular verbs follow a recognizable pattern; irregular verbs must be memorized. With these principal parts, you can create all tenses.
- turn, turned, turned
- yell, yelled, yelled
- sing, sang, sung

2. NOUNS

2.1 There are two types of nouns: abstract and concrete.

- Abstract nouns are not tangible. Your senses cannot detect them. For example, you cannot hold courage or honesty in your hands.
- Concrete nouns are people, places, or things.

2.2 Abstract Nouns:

- The **thoughts** of the great philosopher challenged our **assumptions**.
- The **bravery** of King Leonidas struck **fear** into the hearts of his enemies.
- Solon restructured the Athenian constitution with **skill**.
- I have **reservations** about that.
- My **misery** is only matched by my **poverty**.
- **Honor** comes to the man who displays **integrity**.

2.3 Concrete Nouns:

- He threw the **ball**.
- **Hugo** scored.
- **Penguins** cannot fly, but they waddle well.
- My **mother** cooked the **fish** with the perfect amount of **garlic**, **salt**, and **pepper**.
- I love **books**.
- I dwell in that **building**.

2.4 Nouns can be viewed as either common or proper.

- Common nouns are just as they sound: house, building, pizza, man, air, and paper.
- Proper nouns are specific, usually one-of-a-kind. They are capitalized.
- Dates are also proper nouns.
- Examples: John, King George, 1903, English, Mr. T., New York, World War II.

2.5 Formation of plurals can be tricky.

- Most nouns form their plural by adding s. Desks, tables, and trees.
- If the noun ends in s, sh, x, z, then add "es" to the ending. Gases, taxes, crocuses, and waltzes.

3. ADJECTIVES

3.1 Adjectives modify nouns. They are describing words, which include possessives, articles, demonstratives, indefinites, and numbers.

- **Big** boats sail away into **the** sunset.
- **A black** sea of terror has overwhelmed him. Sophocles, *Oedipus*
- "She is **a** perfectly **terrible** person," said Lucy. C. S. Lewis, *The Lion, The Witch and the Wardrobe*
- **The** ants were **busy** on **the** ground, **big black** ones with **shiny** bodies and **the little dusty quick** ants. John Steinbeck, *The Pearl*

3.2 Possessives:

- **Oedipus's** fault was **his** hubris. (All possessives are adjectives. Whose fault? Oedipus's fault.)
- **His** sight was nothing compared to **Tiresias's** preternatural sight.
- **My** friend lost **his** pen.
- **Our** predicament is not a good one.

Some classify possessives as nouns (genitive case), but in this book we will consider them adjectives.

3.3 Articles will be considered adjectives in this book.

- "Who controls **the** past controls **the** future. Who controls **the** present controls **the** past." George Orwell, *1984*

- Experience is **the** best teacher.
- **The** teacher got into his red Ferrari and revved **the** engine.
- "I am constant as **the** Northern Star." (Northern Star is a noun.) Shakespeare, *Julius Caesar*
- **An** apple **a** day keeps you healthy.

3.4 Demonstrative adjectives modify nouns. The most common ones are this, these, that, and those.

- **That** man over there is my father. ("There" is an adverb.)
- If I hear **those** noises again at midnight, I will run.
- **These** men will go; **those** men will stay.
- Please hand **that** book to me and hand **this** book to Ms. Brooks.

Some classify demonstratives as determiners, but in this book, we will consider them adjectives.

3.5 Indefinite adjectives do not refer to any specific person or thing. Hence, they are indefinite. Typical indefinite pronouns are all, any, each, few, many, none, and some.

- **Many** men will try, but only a **few** men will make it.
- He ate **several** pancakes.
- "**All** animals are equal, but **some** animals are more equal than others." George Orwell, *Animal Farm*
- Cowards die **many** times before their actual death.

3.6 Numbers can be considered special adjectives.

- He sentenced **ten** men to jail.
- In **four** hours, we will be in London.

- **Four** legs good, **two** legs bad. George Orwell, *Animal Farm*
- Numbers always occur before adjectives in a string of words.
- Seven big cats roamed the streets of the city. You cannot say: "Big seven cats…"

3.7 Interrogative adjectives, like other adjectives, modify nouns, but they introduce questions.

In Latin: *qui, quae, quod* = interrogative adjectives. These words are not to be confused with relative pronouns, which share the same forms.

- **What** man will stand for justice?
- **Which** car is the fastest?
- **Whose** father is a consul? This could be written as: The father of whom is a consul?
- **Which** opportunity should I take?

3.8 Some adjectives are irregular in the comparative and superlative. Here are the most common irregular adjectives.

Positive	Comparative	Superlative
Bad	Worse	Worst
Many	More	Most
Well	Better	Best
Little	Less	Least

4. PRONOUNS

4.1 Pronouns take the place of nouns.

- Elijah is an actor. **He** is excellent.
- My mother is a great cook. **She** makes the most amazing peach pie.
- Oranges are delicious. **I** crave **them** all the time.
- John and Joan went to the store. **They** bought candy, chips, and soda.
- Jenny and Michelle should go to the movies. **They** would have a great time.
- Mike and **I** love Shake Shack. **We** are going right after school.

4.2 The antecedent refers to the noun that the pronoun replaces. Since the pronoun replaces the noun, the pronoun must match the noun in number and gender.

- Jim and Jamil went to the movies. **They** (Jim and Jamil) left twenty minutes ago.
- The king bequeathed the land to the Romans. **He** (the king) fulfilled his promise.
- Ms. Smith gave us detention. **She** (Ms. Smith) also yelled at us.
- The cashier gave me the wrong change. **He** (cashier) gave me ten extra dollars.
- I hit the ball into the outfield. **It** (the ball) hit my brother in the head.

4.3 Pronouns:

Subject

	Singular	Plural
1st	I	We
2nd	You	You
3rd	He, She, It	They

Object

	Singular	Plural
1st	Me	Us
2nd	You	You
3rd	Him, Her, It	Them

Reflexive

	Singular	Plural
1st	Myself	Ourselves
2nd	Yourself	Yourselves
3rd	Himself, Herself, Itself	Themselves

4.4 Apart from functioning as subjects, pronouns can be objects and predicate nominatives.

- Rachel gave the book to **him**. (Object of preposition)
- Please hand **him** the keys. (Indirect object)
- Here is the pencil. I'll give **it** to you. (Direct object)
- This is **he**. (Predicate nominative)

4.5 Possessive pronouns. Consider possessive pronouns as adjectives.

- I have **his** book. ("His" is an adjective because it describes what kind of book—his book.)
- **My** cat licked **your** hand. (Whose cat? My cat. Whose hand? Your hand.)
- **Our** friends love playing cards. (Whose friends? Our friends.)
- Who took **my** pencil and **his** Latin book? (Don't be thrown off by questions.)

4.6 Interrogative pronouns ask questions. They are: Who? Whose? Whom? Which? What?

If the question word (Which?) comes before the noun, it becomes an interrogative adjective. If it comes after, it becomes a relative clause/adjective clause.

- **Who** ran for president? Interrogative pronoun.
- **What** did he say? Interrogative pronoun.
- **Which** person ran for president? Interrogative adjective.
- **What** disaster struck the city? Interrogative adjective.
- **Whom** did you see at that party? Interrogative pronoun.
- The book **that** is on the table belongs to my mother. Notice "that" introduces a relative clause/adjective clause.

5. ADVERBS

5.1 Adverbs modify verbs, adjectives, and other adverbs.

- The dog **sadly** whimpered. ("Sadly" modifies "whimpered.")
- The rent is **too** high. ("Too" modifies high.)
- The ninja **very quickly** leapt. ("Very" modifies "quickly," "quickly" modifies "leapt.")
- **Now** is the time to go. ("Now" modifies "is.")
- "I **never** forget a face," my teacher said. ("Never" modifies "forget.")

5.2 Adverbs usually address: when, where, how, and to what degree.

- She ate dinner **early**. (when)
- Lionel Messi kicked the ball **up**. (where)
- The girl studied **diligently**. (how)
- I saw him **yesterday**. (when)
- I'll go **there** with you. (where)
- Stand **up**. (where)
- She was **very** angry. (degree)

5.3 Many adverbs end in "-ly," but not all words that end in "-ly" are adverbs.

- Costly sacrifice – costly is an adjective.
- Deadly force – deadly is an adjective.
- Here are some others: disorderly, ghastly, chilly, bodily, stately, ugly, silly, wily.

- It is worth mentioning that some nouns and verbs also end in "-ly," such as: homily, belly, and supply.
- The bottom line: don't be fooled.

5.4 There are many adverbs that do not have the "-ly" ending.

- Next, forward, not, never, often, always.

5.5 Adverbs also have comparative and superlative forms.

- I watch movies **more frequently** than my brother.
- His dog attacks **most fiercely** when he is hungry.

5.6 The position of the adverb is flexible, but it should be close to the word it modifies.

- Carefully he opened the package.
- He carefully opened the package.

5.7 Conjunctive adverbs connect independent clauses together. The second clause modifies the first. Recognizing them and using them can make your writing more logical.

- Some common conjunctive adverbs: accordingly, also, besides, finally, furthermore, hence, however, indeed, instead, meanwhile, moreover, rather, similarly, then, therefore, thus, and yet.

5.8 Use adverbs sparingly. Strong verbs make for vigorous prose.

The words of Stephen King are apropos. "...[Adverbs are] like dandelions. If you have one on your lawn, it looks pretty unique. If you fail to root it out, however, you find five the next day...fifty the day after that...and then, my brothers and sisters, your lawn is totally, completely, and profligately covered with dandelions. By then you see them for the weeds they really are, but by then it's – GASP!! – too late."

5.9 Some words can be both adverbs and adjectives. Context is key. Ask what word is modified.

- That is a fast car.
- He was driving too fast.
- The early train leaves at noon.
- The train arrive three minutes early.
- That is a hard surface.
- Don't work too hard.

6. PREPOSITIONS

6.1 Prepositional phrases show a relationship within a sentence between the object of the preposition and other words in the sentence.

6.2 Common Prepositions:

About	Below	In	Out
Above	Besides	In front of	Outside
Across	Between	Inside	Over
After	Beyond	In spite of	Regarding
Against	By	Instead of	Since
Along	Concerning	Into	Through
Among	Despite	Like	Throughout
Around	Down	Near	To
At	During	Of	Towards
Because of	Except	On	Under
Before	For	Onto	Up
Behind	From	Out	With / Within / Without

6.3 Prepositions cannot stand by themselves. Prepositions have objects, which are nouns or pronouns.

- Above the table
- Behind the building
- Since the game
- Towards the beach
- Instead of him
- From them

6.4 Choose a word such as "house" as the object of the preposition to determine whether a word is a preposition. This approach will help in most cases.

- About the house, across the house, after the house, against the house, along the house, among the houses, besides the house, by the house, down the house, except the house, regarding the house, etc.

6.5 Certain prepositions can be adverbs or subordinate conjunctions. If there is no *object*, it is an adverb or a subordinate conjunction.

- I stood **up** on the table. ("Up" is an adverb.)
- I wore **out** my pants. ("Out" is an adverb.)
- I looked **up**. ("Up" is an adverb.)
- **Before** I run in the mornings, I eat breakfast. ("Before" is a subordinate conjunction.)

6.6 Some argue that prepositions can take clauses, but in this book, we will make a distinction between subordinate conjunctions and prepositions. The former creates a clause, the latter a phrase.

6.7 A note on style:

Get rid of unnecessary prepositions.

- The boy met **up with** the new students. = The boy met the new students.
- Where are you **at**? = Where arc you?
- It is inside **of** the house. = It is inside the house.

6.8 There are several idiomatic expressions that you need to memorize. In time you will get a sense of these expressions.

- I live on 57th street; I live in an apartment; I live with my family; I live at the end of the road.
- I argue about an issue, I argue with a person; I argue against the law.

7. CONJUNCTIONS

7.1 There are two types of conjunctions.

- Coordinating conjunctions join words, phrases, or clauses.
- Subordinating conjunctions join dependent or subordinate clauses to an independent clause.

7.2 Coordinating conjunctions:

The most common coordinating conjunctions follow the acronym: F-A-N-B-O-Y-S. For, And, Nor, But, Or, Yet, and So.

- He did not want to waste money, **for** he learned the value of making a dollar.
- Caesar was generous **and** merciful.
- Brutus loved Casear, **but** he loved Rome more.
- You may have milk **or** orange juice, not both.
- I won the lottery, **yet** I am not happy.
- General Patton believed in leading by doing, **so** he fought in the fray with his men.

7.3 A note on style:

Even though some shun starting a sentence with "but" and "and," it is acceptable to start a sentence with either conjunction.

- The hawks won the day, as everyone in the senate voted in favor of war. But one voice dissented.

7.4 The most common subordinate conjunctions:

After	Although	As	As if
As long as	As though	Because	Before
Even if	Even though	If	If only
In order that	Rather than	Since	So that
Than	That	Though	Unless
When	Whenever	Where	Whereas
While			

Subordinate conjunctions create subordinate clauses.

- **After I ran the marathon**, I needed rest.
- **Even though I ran the marathon**, I feel fine.
- **Because I left New York**, I miss pizza and bagels.

7.5 Omission of "that." The word "that" may be omitted.

- Artemis knew that Luke would call him after dinner.
- Artemis knew Luke would call him after dinner.
- Luke thought **that** Artemis might be busy.
- Luke thought Artemis might be busy.

Notice that the word "that" is optional.

8. INTERJECTIONS

8.1 Interjections show feelings and bursts of emotions.

- Whoa! That was close.
- Oops, I did it again!
- Zoinks, Scooby!
- Eureka! I found the answer.
- Shhh!
- tut tut
- tsk tsk
- Oh!
- Ouch!
- Gosh!

8.2 Be careful that you do not confuse imperatives and interjections. Imperatives are verbs.

- Sit down!
- Close the door!

8.3 Interjections can take different punctuation marks.

- Huh? What did you mean by that?
- Pssst, pass the sugar.

8.4 With a little practice, you will get the hang of interjections without problems.

PARTS OF SPEECH TEST:

Part I

Underline the nouns in each sentence.

1. A queue of people, huddled and hatted, waited in the hyperborean cold at a new restaurant.
2. The irony of exceptional people is that they do not know they are exceptional and do not seek to be exceptions.
3. This has been a year for the books.

Underline the verbs in each sentence. If there is a linking verb, indicate it.

1. Watch out for the alligators in the river!
2. She became a landscape engineer through sheer effort and dedication to her studies.
3. The sounds of nature give peace to all who listen.

Underline the adjectives in each sentence.

1. The quickest runner in the world is standing over there.
2. Soggy bread never tastes good.
3. One man can do more than ten men if true dedication captures his heart and mind.

Underline the adverbs in each sentence.

1. "Nowadays people know the price of everything and the value of nothing." Oscar Wilde, *Pictures of Dorian Gray*
2. The coach shouted to the player passionately, "Jump up and block the shot."
3. I have not already obtained it, but I press onward and upward to grab hold of it.

Underline the prepositions in each sentence.

1. Nietzsche offers an illustration of a man who hid something behind a bush and goes later to find it. Where is the virtue in that?
2. "He was an old man who fished alone in a skiff in the Gulf Stream, and he had gone eighty-four days now without taking a fish. In the first forty days a boy had been with him." Ernst Hemingway, *The Old Man and the Sea*
3. "Down the face of the precipice, sheer and almost smooth…a small black shape was moving with its thin limbs splayed out." J. R. R. Tolkien, *The Two Towers*

Underline the conjunctions in each sentence and label whether it is a coordinate or subordinate.

1. "Because men, groping in the Arctic darkness, had found a yellow metal, and because steamship and transportation companies were booming the find, thousands of men were rushing into the Northland. These men wanted dogs, and the dogs they wanted were heavy dogs, with strong muscles by which to toil, and furry coats to protect them from the frost." Jack London, *Call of the Wild*
2. "I have made this letter longer than usual, only because I have not had the time to make it shorter." Blaise Pascal
3. "By seven o'clock the orchestra has arrived—no thin five-piece affair but a whole pitful of oboes and trombones and saxophones and viols and cornets and piccolos and low and high drums." Scott Fitzgerald, *The Great Gatsby*

Underline the pronouns in each sentence, drawing arrows to antecedents.

1. He threw a fastball to the catcher, and the batter hit it out of the park.
2. Tim and Grace went to the play together, and they loved it.
3. You said that I said that we saw the movie, but I do not remember it at all.

Underline the interjections in each sentence.

1. Drop the cookie, my man.
2. Yikes, lions, tigers, and bears!
3. He said, "woah, I did not know that I could do that."

Part II

Label the part of speech for every word.

1. Today is a beautiful autumn morning in New York City, leaves in full color, brisk air in my lungs, olive Barbour jackets on Madison Avenue, and an occasional man with a hat.
2. "None of those other things makes a difference. Love is the strongest thing in the world, you know. Nothing can touch it. Nothing comes close. If we love each other, we're safe from it all. Love is the biggest thing there is." David Guterson, *Snow Falling on Cedars*

Part III

Identify the underlined words.

"According to the tradition, **Gyges** was a shepherd in the service of the king of Lydia; there was a great storm, and an earthquake made an opening in the earth at the place where he was feeding **his** flock. Amazed at the sight, he descended into the **opening**, where, among other marvels, he beheld a hollow brazen horse, having doors, at which he stooping and looking in saw a dead body of a corpse, as appeared to him, more than human, and having nothing on but a **gold** ring; this he took from the finger of the dead and re-ascended. **Now** the shepherds met together, according to custom, that they might send their **monthly** report about the flocks to the king; into their assembly he **came** having the ring on his finger, and as he was sitting among them, he chanced to turn the collet of the ring inside his hand, when instantly he became **invisible** to the rest of the company and they began to speak of him as if he were no longer present. He was astonished at this, and again touching the ring he turned the collet outwards and reappeared; he made several **trials** of the ring, and always with the same result-when he turned the collet **inwards,** he became invisible, when outwards he reappeared. Whereupon he contrived to be chosen one of the messengers who were sent to the court; where as soon as he arrived, he seduced the queen, and with her help conspired against the king and slew him **and** took the kingdom. **Suppose** now that there were two such magic rings, and the just put on one of them and the unjust the other; no man can be imagined to be of such an iron nature that he would stand **fast** in justice. No man would keep his hands off what was not his own when he could safely take what he liked out of the market or go into houses and lie with any one at his pleasure, or kill or release from prison whom he would, and in all respects be like a God among men. **Then** the actions of the just would be as the actions of the unjust; they would both come at last to the same point. And this we may truly affirm to be a great proof that a man is just, **not** willingly or because he thinks that justice is any good to him individually, but **of** necessity, for wherever anyone **thinks** that he can safely be unjust, there he is unjust. For all men believe in their hearts that **injustice** is far more profitable to the individual than justice, and he who argues as I have been supposing, will say that they are right. If you could imagine anyone obtaining this power of becoming **invisible**, and never doing any wrong or touching what was another's, he would be thought by the lookers-on to be a most wretched idiot, although they would praise him to one another's faces, and keep **up** appearances with one another from a fear that they too might suffer injustice."

Plato, *Republic*

Do you agree with Glaucon? Will people only act justly when they know someone is watching?

TWO

PARTS OF THE SENTENCE

9. THE PREDICATE

9.1 All sentences must have at least one predicate. The predicate tells what the subject is doing. The verb (action or linking) is the essential part of the predicate. See §1.1-1.9.

9.2 Action:

- I **ran** the marathon.
- Oliver and Walker **won** the game with their teamwork.
- **Stop**!
- They **danced** the night away.
- She **leapt** over the wall.

9.3 Linking:

- We **are** farmers.
- They **are** good sailors.
- She **became** a doctor.
- I **will be** a grammarian.
- The flowers **smell** good.

9.4 Verb phrases contain helping verbs.

- They **will have bought** the present.
- **Would** they **have finished** the assignment?
- The boys **were running** down the hallway.
- **Should** I **run** for office? (Helping verbs can be separated from the main verb.)

9.5 Compound verbs:

- They **will run** and **walk**.
- **Watch** and **learn**.

9.6 Verbs are either passive or active in voice.

- In the active voice, the subject performs the action.
- In the passive voice, the subject receives the action.
- The little girl **ate** the cupcake. Active. The subject performs the action.
- The cupcake **was eaten** by the little girl. The subject receives the action; the cupcake (subject) was eaten.
- The burglar **broke** the door. Active.
- The door **was broken** by the burglar. Passive.

Make these sentences passive:

1. The batter hit the ball out of the park.
2. He whipped the cream to perfection.
3. Bravery won the day.
4. More than other kings, Sargon focused his attention on expansion.
5. The man carried the box of books up the winding stairs.

10. THE SUBJECT

10.1 The best way to find the subject is to first look for the verb of the sentence. Ask who or what is doing the action of the verb.

- **Oedipus** solved the riddle of the sphinx.
- My **brother** loved the novel.
- **Charlie** won the golden ticket.
- **I** pleased my mother with good grades.
- **Christmas** came early this year.
- **He** jumped over the fence, the gate, and the wall.

10.2 If the verb is passive, then the subject receives the action. The thing or person doing the action is usually followed by the preposition "by."

- The **man** was hit by the ball.
- The winning **ticket** was bought by the man.
- The **men** were seen by the enemies.

10.3 Some sentences are imperatival. In these cases, there is an implied "you." The "you" can be either singular or plural.

- Be quiet in the auditorium. (The subject is an implied "you.")
- In the stillness of morning, don't spoil the tranquility. (Don't let the prepositional phrase confuse you. The subject is still an implied "you.")
- Bring the wood from the forest. We need to start a fire.
- Stop it!

- Please pass the sugar.

10.4 When you have a linking verb, the subject is not actually *doing the verb*. Examples will make this point clear.

- **He** is a good boy.
- **Christian** was in school.
- **Creon** and **Jocasta** were in Thebes.
- **He** will be the president of the company.
- The **roses** smell good. (The roses are not sniffing, right?)

10.5 Compound subjects.

- **Snowball** and **Napoleon** were joint leaders of Animal Farm.
- **Atticus** and **Scout** sat under the tree and talked about life.
- **Ozymandias** and **Colossus** had delusions of grandeur.
- **John**, **Max**, **Shelly**, **Ryan**, and **Addie** all came to my place.
- **Rain** and **hail** destroyed our manicured lawn.
- **Strength** and **honor** propelled the legionaries towards audacity.

10.6 Interrogatives. Don't let the question mark at the end of the sentence confuse you. Rewrite the sentence into a declarative, and you will quickly locate the subject.

- Did **E.T.** really phone home? If you make this sentence into a declarative, it will read: "E.T. really did phone home." At this point, the subject is clear.
- How was **Michael Jordan** able to make that incredible shot?

- Do **you** know Babe Ruth's record?
- Did you know that Babe Ruth was married at St. Gregory's Church on W. 90th Street?
- Will **he** arrive on time to catch the show?
- Was the **speech** of the queen inspiring?

10.7 Finally, don't let word order fool you. The verb or other parts of speech can come before the subject. Rewriting the sentence can help in these situations.

- On top of the tower beautifully chimed the **bells**. (The bells on top of the tower chimed beautifully.)
- Hurriedly through the dense forest ran **Robin** towards safety.
- During the plague in Athens **depression** descended.
- Over sea, land, and air ours will be the **victory**.
- Yours are the **trophies**; ours the **glory**. (What is the verb of the second part of the sentence?)

10.8 Appositives always agree in case with the word with which it is in apposition.

- The judge sentenced us—my two friends, my brother, and me.
- My son, Luke, is a lawyer.
- My son, the lawyer, lives in Boston.

10.9 The predicate nominative is not the subject but says something about the subject. It is followed by a linking verb.

- My friend is a **doctor**.
- She became an **actress**.

11. DIRECT OBJECTS

11.1 Direct objects are nouns or pronouns (even clauses) that receive the action of the verb. To locate the direct object, find the verb and ask, "*verb* what or *verb* whom."

- She hit the **ball**. (Hit what? Hit whom? Ball.)
- The boys threw the **can**. (Threw what? Can.)
- Michael crashed the **car**. (Crashed what? Car.)
- Jack played the **drums**. (Played what? Drums.)
- Help **me**! (Help whom? Me.)
- The boys bought **what they wanted**. (Bought what? What they wanted. We will cover noun clauses in §16.)

11.2 In Latin the accusative case is the direct object.

- *Agricolae frumentum portant.* The farmers carry the grain.
- *Nautae viros malos vulneraverunt.* The sailors have wounded the bad men.

11.3 Not all sentences contain a direct object.

- She runs in the park. (Runs what? Runs whom? Nothing makes sense. "Park" is the object of the preposition.)
- The fish swam into the glass of the tank. (Swam what? Swam whom? Nothing makes sense. "Glass" is the object of the preposition.)
- Marcus is a soldier in Caesar's tenth legion. (Tricky. Soldier is a predicate nominative. Predicate nominatives are not direct objects. See §10.9, §16.8.)

11.4 Action verbs are either transitive or intransitive. Transitive verbs can take a direct object and intransitive verbs cannot. Some verbs are both transitive and intransitive. Context is key.

- The dog bumped the boy. (Transitive. Boy = direct object.)
- The boy threw a ball. (Transitive. Ball = direct object.)
- She walks in the garden. (Intransitive. Garden = object of preposition.)
- He walks the dog in the park. (Transitive. Dog = direct object.)
- She stands on the mountain. (Intransitive. No direct object. Mountain = object of the preposition.)
- She stands the book on the table. (Transitive. Book = direct object.)

11.5 General Formula. Subject + Verb + What? / Whom? = Direct Object.

- This formula works not only with nouns and pronouns but also clauses. See §16 for a discussion on noun clauses.
- Achilles threw the **javelin,** and it hit the **man** on the horse.
- Dr. Seuss wrote my favorite **books**.
- She gave **what she wanted to give**. ("What she wanted to give" is a noun clause.)
- She hopes **that he will come home**. ("That he will come home" is a noun clause.)

12. INDIRECT OBJECTS

12.1 An indirect object tells to or for whom or what the action of the verb has been done. The indirect object comes before the direct object. To find the indirect object, ask to or for whom. Examples will make this point clear.

- The teacher gave **me** the answer. (Gave what? The answer. To whom? Me)
- The magnanimous donor gave the **school** a check for a hundred million dollars. (Gave what? A check. To whom or what? The school)
- The father threw **me** the ball. (Threw what? The ball. To whom? Me)
- I told **you** the truth. (Told what? The truth. To whom? You)
- The painter showed the **audience** his magnum opus. (Showed what? His magnum opus. To whom? the audience)

12.2 In Latin the case of the indirect object is the dative.

- *Donum tibi dedi.* I gave you the gift.

12.3 Indirect objects can be made into prepositional phrases. Latin students, proceed with caution. In English, prepositional phrases are not indirect objects though they can replace the indirect object.

- The teacher gave the answer **to me**.

- The magnanimous donor gave a check for a hundred million dollars **to the school**.
- The father threw the ball **to me**.
- I told the truth **to you**.
- The painter showed his magnum opus **to the audience**.

12.4 Indirect objects are moderately rare. In order to have an indirect object, you need a transitive verb and a direct object. Without both, you cannot have an indirect object.

12.5 Common verbs that have indirect objects.

- Buy, get, cook, bring, give, lend, offer, pass, send, show, and promise.

13. PREPOSITIONAL PHRASES

13.1 Common Prepositions:

About	Below	In	Out
Above	Besides	In front of	Outside
Across	Between	Inside	Over
After	Beyond	In spite of	Regarding
Against	By	Instead of	Since
Along	Concerning	Into	Through
Among	Despite	Like	Throughout
Around	Down	Near	To
At	During	Of	Towards
Because of	Except	On	Under
Before	For	Onto	Up
Behind	From	Out	With / Within / Without

13.2 Prepositions cannot stand by themselves. Prepositions have objects, which are nouns or pronouns.

- Behind the garden
- Before the garden
- Under the garden
- Within the garden
- From the garden

13.3 Prepositions are either adjectival or adverbial. If a prepositional phrase is adjectival, it will modify a noun or a pronoun; if it is adverbial, it will modify a verb, adjective, or another adverb.

13.4 Adjectival prepositional phrases usually answer the question "which one." If you can make the prepositional phrase into a relative clause, you are dealing with an adjectival prepositional phrase.

- The cup **on the stand** contains milk. (The cup, which is on the stand, contains milk. Which cup? The one on the stand.)
- The wolves **of the forest** howl. (The wolves, which are of the forest, howl. Which wolves? The ones in the forest.)
- The delegates **from New England** were pleasant. (The delegates, who are from New England, were pleasant. Which delegates? The ones from New England.)
- The strawberries **in my mother's** garden are the best I've ever eaten. (The strawberries, which are in my mother's garden, are the best I've ever eaten. Which strawberries? The ones in my mother's garden.)

13.5 Adverbial prepositional phrases usually answer the questions: **how, when, or where.**

- She ran **into the bathroom** because she had a bloody nose. (Where? "Into the bathroom" modifies "ran.")
- The mouse scurried **underneath the train tracks** never to be seen again. (Where? "Underneath the train tracks" modifies "scurried.")
- **During the play** Jeff yawned. (When? "During the play" modifies "yawn")

- **After dinner** we chatted **for hours**. (When? "After dinner" modifies "chatted.")
- The car sped **with great skill**. (How? "With great skill" modifies "sped."

14. APPOSITIVES

14.1 Appositives occur when two or more nouns are placed next to each other and refer to the same thing. What comes after the first noun is in apposition. It gives further information. Examples will make this point clear.

- My son, **a lawyer**, lives in New York.
- On our way to Philadelphia, we stopped by Cherry Hill, **a sleepy suburb in New Jersey.**

14.2 Do no confuse appositives with items in a list.

- In college, I lived in a camped off-campus apartment with Jeff, John, and Matt.
- Note that Jeff, John, and Matt are in a list.

14.3 Appositives are akin to relative clauses without the relative pronoun.

- The coffee shop, a hole in the wall, serves the best cup of cappuccino.
- The coffee shop, which is a hole in the wall, serves the best cup of cappuccino.

14.4 Appositives often comprise of phrases, not just a single word.

- I saw a rare bird in the park, **a beautiful red-tailed hawk with a field mouse in his claws.**

PARTS OF THE SENTENCE TEST:

Part I
Underline the subjects.

1. There is a dark side when efficiency becomes the lens through which we look at everything.
2. Even Adam Smith, the father of capitalism and a proponent of efficiency, believed that there was something more important than efficiency in an economy. For him, it was morality.
3. "It sounds plausible enough tonight but wait until tomorrow. Wait for the common sense of the morning." H. G. Wells, *The Time Machine*

Underline the direct objects.

1. He became the CEO of the company when he exerted intelligence, charm, and hard work to every endeavor.
2. Francis Bacon, an unabashed admirer of Machiavelli, took cues from him and applied it to scientific inquiry as he forced nature to give up her secrets.
3. "The general filled both glasses, and said, 'God makes some men poets. Some He makes kings, some beggars. Me He made a hunter.'" Richard Connell, "The Most Dangerous Game"

Underline the indirect objects.

1. Amoebaean singing is not something that is familiar to most Americans, but it was common in the Hellenistic world.
2. The mother said, "Give it a try; fortune favors bravery."

Underline the prepositional phrases.

1. If we parse the logic of the first set of quatrains, there is an arresting insight.
2. All we need to do is to look at the remains of inscriptions, statues, coins, and busts; all these artifacts are ancient marks of a society obsessed with honor. The more the better.
3. Had Twitter existed in the fourteenth century, Robert Holcot, a scholastic philosopher, would have thumbed on his iPhone: "to do what lies within you." His tonsured companions would have appreciated his economic use of language to make such a profound point.

Part II

Identify the underlined words.

A Mexican American Explores Multiculturalism

"The other day, the **phone** rang; it was a **woman** who identified herself as the 'talent coordinator' for the 'Oprah Winfrey Show.' She said Oprah was planning a show on self-hating ethnics. 'You know,' she confided, 'Norwegians who don't want to be Norwegian, Greeks who hate Greek food.' Anyway, she said **breezily**, wouldn't I like to make an appearance?

About 10 years ago I wrote a thin book called *Hunger of Memory*. It was a book about my education, which is to say, a book about my **Americanization**. I wrote of losses and **triumphs**. And, in passing, I wrote about two issues particularly, affirmative action and bilingual education.

I was a naysayer. I became, because of my book, a notorious figure among the Ethnic Left in America. Consider me the brown Uncle Tom. I am a traitor, a sell-out. The Spanish word is *pocho*. A *pocho* is someone who forgets his true home.

Last year, I was being interviewed by Bill Moyers. 'Do you consider yourself American or Hispanic?' he asked. 'I think of myself as Chinese,' I answered.

A **smart-aleck** answer, but one that is true enough. I live in San Francisco, a city that has become, in my lifetime, predominantly Asian, predominantly Chinese. I am becoming like **them**. Do not ask me how, it is too early to tell. But it is inevitable, living side by side, that we should become like each other. So, think of me as Chinese.

Oh, my critics say: Look at you **Mr. Rod-ree-guess**. You have lost your culture.

They mean, I think, that I am not my father, which is true enough. I did not grow up in the state of Jalisco, in the western part of Mexico. I grew up here, in this country, amongst you. I am like you.

My critics mean, when they speak of culture, something solid, something intact. You have lost your culture, they say, as though I lost it at the Greyhound bus station. You have lost your culture, as though culture is a **coat** I took off one warm afternoon and then forgot.

I AM MY CULTURE. Culture is not something opposite us, it is rather something we breathe and sweat and live. My culture? Lucille Ball **is** my culture. (I love Lucy, after all.) And Michael Jackson. And Benjamin Franklin is my culture. And Elvis Presley and Walter Cronkite. Walt Disney is my culture. The New York Yankees.

My culture is **you**. You created me; if you don't like **it**, if I make you uncomfortable **now** by being too much like you, too bad."

Richard Rodriguez, "The Chinese in All of Us"

Do you agree with Richard Rodriguez's sentiments?

Part III

1. Write a sentence with an introductory prepositional phrase and an indirect object.

2. Write a sentence with a predicate nominative and an indirect object.

THREE

CLAUSES

15. CLAUSES

15.1 A clause has a subject and a verb unlike a phrase which has no subject or verb. Clauses can be independent or dependent/subordinate.

- When I came home... (Dependent)
- After John and Jane ate dinner... (Dependent)
- The boys ran the race. (Independent)

15.2 An independent clause is a group of words that contains a subject and a verb and can stand by itself.

- She sang a beautiful song.
- The construction workers razed the building.
- The computer broke.

15.3 A dependent clause is a group of words that contains a subject and verb, but the clause cannot stand alone. It requires an independent clause to complete the sentence.

- Since I ate lunch...
- Whenever I read *To Kill a Mockingbird*...
- Because I finished my project...
- Although I am tired...
- Since I ate lunch, I am not hungry.
- Whenever I read *To Kill a Mockingbird*, I remember 7th grade.
- Because I finished my project, I am going to the movies.
- Although I am tired, I will continue to work.

15.4 There are three types of sentences: simple, compound, and complex. Simple sentences have one independent clause. Compound sentences have at least two independent clauses. Complex sentences have at least one dependent and one independent clause.

- Michael plays the drums. (simple)
- Michael plays the drums, but Gabriel plays the bass. (compound)
- When Michael plays the drums, Gabriel plays the bass. (complex)
- Michael plays the drums, and Gabriel plays the bass whenever they come together. (compound-complex sentence)

15.5 There are three types of subordinate clauses: adjectival, adverbial, and noun clauses. We will only cover the first two for now.

15.6 An adjectival clause modifies or describes a noun or pronoun.

- The man, **who is standing there**, is my professor. (Which man? The one over there.)
- James, **whom you saw at the party**, is going to Yale next year to study history. (Which James? The one you saw at the party.)
- Here comes the CEO **by whom the company was restructured**. (Which CEO? The one by whom the company was restructured.)
- This is the book **that I love**. (Which book? The one I love.)

- This is the book **I love**. (Notice that "that" may be omitted.)

Think of the relative clause in Latin.

- *Vidi eos qui ad insulam navigaverunt.* I saw those who sailed to the island.
- *Imperator cui periculum nuntiatum est milites ad castra duxit.* The general to whom the danger was announced led the soldiers to the camp.
- *Qui pecuniam dat bonus amicus est.* He who gives money is a good man.

15.7 An adverbial clause, like an adverb, modifies verbs, adjectives, or adverbs. It is introduced by a subordinate conjunction, such as: if, when, because, until, while, etc.

- **Whenever the markets tumble**, I take a deep breath and take a walk.
- **Because she was late for a month**, the company fired her.
- **After I get ready for bed**, I read a chapter of my favorite author.
- **Since taking my vacation**, I feel like a new woman.
- **If I work diligently**, I will succeed. Keep in mind that conditionals ("if" and "unless") introduce adverbial clauses.
- Adverbial clauses can also come after the main clause. When this happens, no comma is needed. I take a deep breath and take a walk **whenever the markets tumble**.

15.8 Adverbial clauses cannot be the object of a preposition.

- It is like ~~when you fall and get hurt~~.
- It is like falling and getting hurt.

15.9 Adverbial clauses cannot be predicate nominatives.

- The reason I love New York City is ~~because there is so much to see and do~~.
- The reason I love New York City is that there is so much to see and do.

EXERCISES:

Draw parentheses around dependent clauses and identify the type—adjectival or adverbial. If there is a noun clause, be sure to label its function. The following are the first sentences of works of literature.

1. "Sing, goddess, the anger of Peleus' son Achilles and its devastation, which put pains thousandfold upon the Achaians, hurled in their multitudes to the house of Hades…" Homer, *Iliad*
2. "Tell me, Muse, of the man of many ways, who was driven far journeys, after he had sacked Troy's sacred citadel." Homer, *Odyssey*
3. "Son of Laertes! I have always seen you hunt to seize some quick advantage over enemies; and now I see you at the

seashore house of Aias, where he has the last position on the flank." Sophocles, *Aias*

4. "There is an old saying that runs like this: You cannot be sure that someone has had a good or bad life until he is dead." Sophocles, *Women of Trachis*

5. "When he was nearly thirteen, my brother Jem got his arm badly broken at the elbow. When it healed, and Jem's fears of never being able to play football were assuaged, he was seldom self-conscious about his injury." Harper Lee, *To Kill a Mockingbird*

6. "If we are going to look for the most primitive and simple religion which we can observe, it is necessary to begin by defining what is meant by religion." Emile Durkheim, *The Elementary Forms of the Religious Life*

7. "I was born a slave on a plantation in Franklin County, Virginia. I am not quite sure of the exact place or exact date of my birth, but at any rate I suspect I must have been born somewhere and at some time." Booker T. Washington, *Up From Slavery*

8. "In my younger and more vulnerable years my father gave me some advice that I've been turning over in my mind ever since." F. Scott Fitzgerald, *The Great Gatsby*

9. "Don't be afraid. My telling can't hurt you in spite of what I have done, and I promise to lie quietly in the dark—weeping perhaps or occasionally seeing the blood once more—but I

will never again unfold my limbs to rise up and bare teeth." Toni Morrison, *A Mercy*

10. "Starting out on the biography of my hero, Alexei Fyodorovich Karamazov, I find myself in some perplexity. Namely, that while I do call Alexei Fyodorovich my hero, still, I myself know that he is by no means a great man, so that I can foresee the inevitable questions, such as: What is notable about your Alexei Fyodorovich that you should choose him for your hero?" Fyodor Dostoevsky, *The Brothers Karamazov*

CLAUSE PRACTICE:

How many clauses are in each sentence? Also identify the type of sentence (simple, complex, compound, compound-complex).

1. The woman caught a glimpse of the thief before he put on his disguise, but she could not identify him because three other men had the same statue and the same shade of hair color. ______________________________

   ____

2. If she is who she says she is, then she is of German royalty, but if she is lying, then she is the daughter of an accountant from New Jersey. ______________________________

3. Because of the fog, the plane could not take off. ________

   ____

4. On account of the virus, the university decided to shut down the spring term even amid the protests. ________________

____

5. In order to find the perfect apartment, which appeared in a dream, the couple walked every inch of the city and failed.

____

6. When you visit New York City, make sure to visit the restaurant where we first had a cup of coffee. __________

____

7. The young trader committed a grave mistake when he sold the wrong stock at the wrong price on the wrong day. ___

____

8. The shirt I love was drenched in the downpour, but the shirt I despise sits on my shelf in pristine condition.

____

9. On entering the room, Andreas threw his cap onto the chair as he proceeded toward the kitchen to grab a coke from the refrigerator. ________________________________

____

10. I love it when it pours, but my house leaks. _____________

____

WRITING CLAUSES:

Write two sentences with adjectival clauses. The adjectival clause must modify the DO.

1. ______________________________

____

____

____

____

____

____

2. ______________________________

____

____

____

____

____

____

Write two sentences with adverbial clauses in a compound-complex sentence.

1. ____

2. ____

16. NOUN CLAUSES

16.1 A noun clause is a clause (has a subject and verb), but it functions as a noun. Often the noun clause can be replaced with the word, "it."

16.2 Clauses as nouns:

- Taco Bell made me sick. (Taco Bell is clearly the subject.)
- **What I ate** made me sick. (What I ate = noun clause = subject.)
- I love Taco Bell. (Taco Bell is the direct object.)
- I love **what my mother makes**. (What my mother makes = noun clause = direct object.)
- I will give Taco Bell a try. (Taco Bell is the indirect object.)
- I will give whatever you give me a try. (Whatever you give me = noun clause = indirect object.)

Use the substitution method. Replace the noun clause with a noun or pronoun to see if it makes sense.

16.3 Wherever you have a noun, it can be replaced with a noun clause. This means that noun clauses can be subjects, direct objects, indirect objects, objects of a preposition, predicate nominatives, and appositives.

16.4 Subjects:

- **What I made** pleased my family.

- **How we got the piano into that narrow door** boggles my mind.
- **How he gives** inspires me.

16.5 Direct objects:

- I love **whatever he does**.
- I hate **that I love you**.
- Ask **what he wants for his birthday**.

16.6 Indirect objects:

- I will give **whatever my mother asks me** a try.
- Your parents will probably give **what you desire** some thought.
- The judge will give **what the defense said** serious consideration.

16.7 Object of Preposition:

- He never cares about **what the people think**.
- From **where I am standing**, I cannot see the opera.
- Did the conduct committee punish the boys for **how they behaved**?

16.8 Predicate Nominative:

- I am **what I eat**.
- The situation is **that you don't have any money**.
- A computer is **what I wanted for Christmas**.

16.9 Appositive:

- The problem, **that you lost your keys twice**, is bothersome.
- The suggestion, **that you do your work well in advance**, is a good one.

16.10 When a sentence starts with "it" and does not have an antecedent, then "it" is not a subject pronoun. It is a placeholder, and the noun clause is the subject.

Examples will make this point clearer.

- It is sad that I have to repeat myself = That I have to repeat myself is sad.
- It is true that he did it = That he did it is true.
- Is it a proven fact that elephants have good memories? That elephants have good memories is a proven fact. (Notice that the interrogative has been made into a declarative sentence).
- It is great that he is coming to the party = That he is coming to the party is great.
- It was a shock that the Mets won that game in the ninth inning = That the Mets won that game in the ninth inning was a shock.

EXERCISES:

Underline the noun clauses and identify how they are used.

1. I loved what the chef made.
2. The students complained about how difficult the test was.

3. When you are in a foreign country, you should try what the locals eat.
4. What did I say?
5. Give whatever she made a try; you might like it.
6. Sharks that swim in cold waters love spicy tuna.
7. Don't forget to send a thank you note to whoever interviewed you.
8. How the director shot the film still amazes me.
9. What is done is done.
10. If you come to my apartment, we can eat what my mother used to make in the old country.
11. Whoever thought of that idea is a veritable genus.
12. Choose a gift for whomever you desire.
13. I'll take two of whatever he just had.
14. After a detention it is important to think about what you could have done differently.
15. I always wonder about what will happen if I am stranded on an island.
16. On Saturdays we can do whatever we want within parental parameters from noon to midnight.
17. Why do you ask about why we have to do the work?
18. He is what I imagined him to be.
19. Whatever you say is true.

20. What has been done cannot be undone.

LABEL CLAUSES:

Draw parentheses around subordinate clauses and draw arrows where appropriate. If there is a noun clause, label its grammatical function (S, DO, IO, PN, OP, and APP).

1. What I have done I did because it was the best option available at the time.
2. If the game is delayed any further, we will have to play two games tomorrow.
3. I ate what my father packed for lunch, all of it, even the broccoli that I really do not like.
4. "But, first, remember, remember, remember the signs. Say them to yourself when you wake in the morning and when you lie down at night, and when you wake in the middle of the night." C. S. Lewis, *The Silver Chair*
5. I love the book he wrote, but what he wrote sometimes confused me even to the point that I put the book down for two months.
6. "History, Stephen said, is a nightmare from which I am trying to awake." James Joyce, *Ulysses*
7. He who has ears let him hear what the Spirit says to the churches.

8. Please give whatever he says a try; it won't be worse than what will happen if you do nothing.

9. Wandering across the forest, the man saw a tree that reaches the heavens and whose leaves bring healing to the nations.

10. "What book do we need to read for homework?" bellowed the boy who barely spoke in class.

ADDITIONAL EXERCISE:

1. "If one of them suggested sowing a bigger acreage with barley, the other was certain to demand a bigger acreage of oats, and if one of them said that such and such a field was just right for cabbages, the other would declare that it was useless for anything except roots." George Orwell, *Animal Farm*

2. "I have promised that someone should watch for him and give him instant notice if any new object should appear in sight." Upton Sinclair, *The Jungle*

3. "I beheld, then, that they all went on till they came to the foot of the Hill Difficulty; at the bottom of which was a spring." John Bunyan, *Pilgrim's Progress*

4. "Now, just after sundown, when all my work was over and I was on my way to my berth, it occurred to me that I should like an apple." Robert Louis Stevenson, *Treasure Island*

5. "It is much better to do good in a way that no one knows anything about it." Leo Tolstoy, *Anna Karenina*

17. WHO AND WHOM

Deciding between who/whom does not have to be difficult. With a little practice, you will master the difference. Read through the following steps and practice.

17.1 Isolate the clause or phrase.

- Once you find the who/whom clause or phrase, ask what the clause or phrase requires.
- If the clause or phrase requires a subject, then "who" is correct.
- If the clause or phrase requires an object, then "whom" is correct.
- To who/whom will she give the book? "To" introduces a prepositional phrase, which means you need an object. "Whom" is correct.
- Who/whom will manage the company? "Who" is correct because you need a subject.

17.2 Substitution Method:

- The easiest way to determine whether who/whom is correct, substitute he/him or she/her.
- If the sentence is an interrogative, then turn it into a declarative sentence, and then use the substitution method.

EXAMPLES:

- You covered that story about who/whom? = Did you cover that story about he/him? "Him" is obviously the choice.
- For who/whom will she postpone the flight? = She will postpone the flight for he or him. "Him" is the clear choice.

17.3 More Difficult Sentences:

- Predicate Nominative. Try this one: Do you know who/ whom I am?
- The answer is actually "who," because the verb "am" is a linking verb that requires a predicate nominative.

17.4 The hardest sentences are those that have a conflict of interest—the who/whom plays a roles in two clauses. In other words, who/whom plays a role in the main clause and the dependent clause. In these cases, the dependent clause wins.

- Try this one. Just hurry up and pass the ball to whoever/ whomever is open. Since "to whoever/whomever is open" is the dependent clause, it wins out. "Whoever" is the correct answer.

WHO/WHOM PRACTICE:

Circle either **who** or **whom.**

1. **Who/whom** died and made you king?

2. **Who/whom** did the Jets play last night?
3. I wasn't startled because I know **who/whom** you are.
4. Did you hear about the seventh-grade boy **who/whom** swallowed a bug?
5. **Who/whom** did he think I threw it to?
6. You wrote an article about **who/whom?**
7. The shark will eat **whoever/whomever** it desires.
8. **Whoever/whomever** told you it was okay to play with your phone in class was mistaken!
9. We all wondered **who/whom** the customer bribed to get such excellent service.
10. Consider **who/whom** you'd like to play on your team.
11. Confused at the chairman's urging to censor the official, the trustee bellowed, "Stop **who/whom**?"
12. My brother wondered **who/whom** was waiting outside?
13. **Who/whom** shall I send?
14. Do you know **who/whom** was elected as the president of the United States?
15. I would have spoken sooner, but I was not sure to **who/whom** the question was directed.
16. Before giving out seconds on dessert, figure out **who/whom** wants some.

17. Just hurry up and pass the ball to **whoever/whomever** is open.

18. "Darcy, on the contrary, had seen a collection of people in **who/whom** there was little beauty and no fashion, for none of **who/whom** he had felt the smallest interest, and from none received either attention or pleasure. Miss Bennet he acknowledged to be pretty, but she smiled too much. Mrs. Hurst and her sister allowed it to be so—but still they admired her and liked her, and pronounced her to be a sweet girl, and one **who/whom** they would not object to know more of. Miss Bennet was therefore established as a sweet girl, and their brother felt authorized by such commendation to think of her as he chose." Jane Austen, *Pride and Prejudice*

WHO/WHOM PRACTICE:

Circle either **who** or **whom.**

1. **Who/Whom** knows the answer to the riddle of the Sphinx?
2. He married **who/whom**?
3. I know **who/whom** you are!
4. **Who/Whom** do you think you are?
5. **Who/Whom** goes there?
6. I scored better than **who/whom**?
7. You'd better clearly say **who/whom** you want to ask.

8. **Who/whom** wants some candy?
9. It is not what you know; it is **who/whom** you know.
10. **Whoever/whomever** loves his life will lose it; **Whoever/whomever** loses his life will find it.

ADDITIONAL EXERCISES:

1. Mr. Green spent a good deal of his time worrying about his sons, **who/whom** he feared would disappoint him.
2. "This is the interpretation of Jerome, whose words they have quoted in their canons. But as regards those to **who/whom** they apply the passage, if they wish the landmarks to be fixed, why do they, whenever it suits their purpose, so freely overleap them? Among the Fathers there were two, the one of **who/whom** said, 'Our God neither eats nor drinks, and therefore has no need of chalices and salvers;' and the other 'Sacred rites do not require gold, and things which are not bought with gold, please not by gold.'" John Calvin, *Institutes of Religion*

18. TYPES OF SENTENCES

18.1 There are four types of sentences: simple, compound, complex, and compound complex.

18.2 Simple sentences have one independent clause.

- The car careened off the road.
- The teacher handed out the test.

18.3 Compound sentences have at least two independent clauses.

- The car careened off the road, but the driver avoided the tree.
- The teacher handed out the test, and the students received them.

18.4 Complex sentences have an independent clause and at least one dependent clause.

- Although the car careened off the road, the driver avoided the tree.
- When the teacher handed out the tests, the students were excited.

18.5 Compound complex sentences have at least two independent clause and one dependent clause.

- Although the car careened off the road, the driver avoided the tree, but the cow was not so lucky.

- When the teacher handed out the tests, the students were excited, and they cheered.

Identify how many clauses each sentence has and label what kind of sentence it is. David Foster Wallace's words to Kenyon College graduates—adapted. Feel free to jot down notes in the extra space.

1. There are these two young fish swimming along, and they happen to meet an older fish swimming the other way, who nods at them and says, "Morning, boys. How's the water?"

____

____

____

____

2. The point of the fish story is merely that the most obvious, important realities are often the ones that are hardest to see and talk about.

____

____

____

____

3. Here is just one example of the total wrongness of something I tend to be automatically sure of: everything in my own immediate experience supports my deep belief that I am the absolute center of the universe.

4. If you worship money and things, if they are where you tap real meaning in life, then you will never have enough, never feel you have enough.

5. Worship your body and beauty and allure and you will always feel ugly, and when time and age start showing, you will die a million deaths before they finally grieve you.

6. Worship power, you will end up feeling weak and afraid, and you will need ever more power over others to numb you to your own fear.

7. Worship your intellect, being seen as smart, you will end up feeling stupid, a fraud, always on the verge of being found out.

____

____

____

____

____

8. It is about the real value of a real education, which has almost nothing to do with knowledge, and everything to do with simple awareness; awareness of what is so real and essential, so hidden in plain sight all around us, all the time, that we have to keep reminding ourselves over and over.

____

____

____

____

____

David Foster Wallace, Commencement Speech,
Kenyon College, 2005

The speech ends in this way.

"This is water."

"This is water."

It is unimaginably hard to do this, to stay conscious and alive in the adult world day in and day out. Which means yet another grand cliché turns out to be true: your education really IS the job of a lifetime. And it commences: now.

I wish you way more than luck.

Do you agree with David Foster Wallace that the most obvious things are the most difficult to see? Why?

CLAUSE TEST:

Part I

Draw parentheses around adjectival clauses.

1. The Romans restored to the Locrians what had been taken away, paid twice the money that was taken from the temple, performed expiatory rites after inquiring to whom expiation should be made and in what manner, and finally removed the Roman soldiers who were implicated in the crimes at Locri.
2. The book of ancient lore that lays on the desk belongs to my grandfather who found it in a cave near the site of Knossos in Crete.
3. I shall never forget the first restaurant where I ate chicken tikka masala.

Draw parentheses around adverbial clauses.

1. The Romans were unapologetically concerned with the gods. Indeed, if one trusts the ancient sources, the Romans were famous for, or better yet made famous by their piety towards the gods.
2. "I can see the sun, but even if I cannot see the sun, I know that it exists." Fyodor Dostoevsky, *The Brothers Karamazov*

3. “The people of the village began to gather in the square, between the post office and the bank, around ten o’clock; in some towns there were so many people that the lottery took two days and had to be started on June 2nd.” Shirley Jackson, “The Lottery”

Draw parentheses around noun clauses.

1. That it snowed in April does not surprise me, but what does surprise me is that the administration did not close school or even give a delayed opening.
2. It might seem odd that critics view her as the greatest athlete, but she won three championships in three different sports, what no one has done before.
3. “He examined the ground closely and found what he had hoped to find—the print of hunting boots. They pointed along the cliff in the direction he had been going. Eagerly he hurried along, now slipping on a rotten log or a loose stone but making headway; night was beginning to settle down on the island.” Richard Connell, “The Most Dangerous Game”

Part II

Draw parentheses around all subordinate clauses, drawing arrow where appropriate.

1. No matter how great the inversions are in these plays, they are make-believe and temporary; traditional roles are reestablished as soon as the play is over.
2. Ms. Mitchell said that what she read was the best piece of creative writing that she had ever seen.
3. "I know not all that may be coming, but be it what it will, I'll go to it laughing." Herman Melville, *Moby Dick*

Part III
Identify the underlined clauses and words.

<u>When he gave us our air-rifles</u>, Atticus wouldn't teach us to shoot. Uncle Jack instructed **<u>us</u>** in the rudiments thereof; he said Atticus wasn't interested in guns. Atticus said to Jem one day, "I'd rather you shot at tin cans in the backyard, but I know you'll go after birds. Shoot all the bluejays you want, **<u>if you can hit 'em</u>**, but remember it's a sin to kill a mockingbird."

That was the only time I ever heard Atticus say it was a sin to do something, and I asked Miss Maudie about it.

"Your father's right," she said. "Mockingbirds don't do one thing **<u>but</u>** make music for us to enjoy. They don't eat up people's gardens, don't nest in corncribs, they don't do one thing but sing their hearts out for us. That's **<u>why it's a sin to kill a mockingbird</u>**."

"Miss Maudie, this is an old neighborhood, ain't it?"

"Been here longer than the town."

"Nome,[2] I mean the folks on our street are all old. Jem and me's the only **children** around here. Mrs. Dubose is close on to a hundred and Miss Rachel's old and so are you and Atticus."

"I don't call fifty very old," said Miss Maudie tartly. "Not being wheeled around yet, am I? Neither's your **father**. But I must say Providence was kind enough to burn down that old mausoleum of mine, I'm **too** old to keep it up—maybe you're right, Jean Louise, this is a settled neighborhood. You've never been around young folks much, have you?"

"Yessum, at school."

"I mean young grown-ups. You're lucky, you know. You and Jem have the benefit of your father's age. **If your father was thirty**, you'd find life quite different."

"I sure would. Atticus can't do anything..."

"You'd be surprised," said Miss Maudie. "There's life in him yet."
"What can he do?"

"Well, he can make somebody's will so airtight can't anybody meddle with it." "Shoot..."

"Well, did you know **he's the best checker-player in this town**? Why, down at the Landing **when we were coming up**, Atticus Finch could beat everybody on both sides of the river."

"Good Lord, Miss Maudie, Jem and me beat him all the time."

"It's about time you found out **it's because he lets you**....

I went to the back yard and found Jem plugging away at a tin can, **which seemed stupid with all the bluejays around.** I

---

2 A blending of "no ma'am."

returned to the front yard and busied myself for two hours erecting a complicated breastworks at the side of the porch, consisting of a tire, an orange crate, the laundry hamper, the porch chairs, and a small U.S. flag Jem gave me from a popcorn box.

When Atticus came home to dinner, he found me crouched down aiming across the street. "What are you shooting at?"

"Miss Maudie's rear end."

Atticus turned and saw my generous target bending over her bushes. He pushed his hat to the back of his head and crossed the street. "Maudie," he called, "I thought **I'd better warn you.** You're in considerable peril."

Miss Maudie straightened up and looked toward me. She said, "Atticus, you are a devil from hell."

When Atticus returned, he told me to break camp. "Don't you ever let me catch you pointing that gun at anybody again," he said.

Harper Lee, *To Kill a Mockingbird*

FOUR

VERBALS

19. GERUNDS

19.1 Gerunds are verbal nouns. Like verbs they can take adverbial modifiers and objects, but they function as nouns.

19.2 Gerunds end in –ing. However, not all words that end in –ing are gerunds.

- **Studying** is a virtue.
- **Running** a marathon is not easy.
- I gave **playing** the violin my greatest effort.
- My parents have a swimming pool in their backyard. (Note: "swimming" ends in "ing," but it is not a gerund. It is an adjective.)
- The officer gave me a speeding ticket. (Again "speeding" is not a gerund.)
- Nothing interests me. ("Nothing" is a noun.)

19.3 Gerunds can function in all the ways nouns can. This means that they can be subjects, direct objects, indirect objects, objects of prepositions, predicate nominatives, and appositives.

- **Running** is my favorite sport. (Subject)
- I like **eating** good foods. (Direct object)
- The boy gave **studying** Latin his best effort. (Indirect object)
- Without **staying** on course, you will veer off the narrow path. (Object of the preposition)
- Her desire was **winning** at all costs. (Predicate nominative)

- His new job, **testing** game consoles for money, is unbelievable. (Appositive)

19.4 Since gerunds are *verbal* nouns, words can modify gerunds (adverbs and adjectives), and they can take objects.

- **Running a company** takes intelligence, effort, and good luck. ("Company" is the object of "running.")
- I enjoy **taking brisk walks** at the crack of dawn. ("Walks" is the object of "taking." "Taking" is the direct object of the sentence.)
- **By struggling constantly**, the men have developed character and stamina. ("Constantly" is the adverb that modifies "struggling." "Struggling is the object of the preposition")
- **Productively managing time** is a skill that great men and women learn. ("Productively" modifies "managing" and "time" is the object of "managing.")
- **His skillful explaining of grammar** made my life easier. ("Skillful" modifies "explaining.")

*A special note: an adjective with a gerund is stylistically pleasant.

- **Giving him money** is probably not the best idea. ("Him" is the indirect object; "Money" = object)

Try these:

- Writing essays requires time and effort.
- Cultivating the mind is as necessary as eating food for the body.
- Nothing gets done by complaining.

19.5 The gerund phrase includes all objects and modifiers.

- **Traveling lightly** is wise when you go hiking.
- **Looking for your ring on the beach** is an impossible task. ("On the beach" is a prepositional phrase, but it is an adverbial phrase that modifies the gerund, "looking.")
- **By riding your bicycle on the right side of the road**, you limit the dangers of oncoming traffic.
- I do not like **wasting the time of others**.
- Nicholas might be in trouble **for failing to hand in his homework**. ("To hand" is an infinitive. We will get to infinitives in a subsequent section.)

EXERCISES:

Underline the gerund/gerund phrases and label how they are used (S, DO, IO, OP, PN, APP).

1. Running on three hours of sleep caused the student to drool on his desk.
2. Without preparing for exams, you will probably fail and cause short-term suffering.
3. He was swimming in the lake when he realized that his doctor forbid swimming for three months.
4. "It is like trying to find a needle in a haystack!" said the teacher.
5. He likes eating ice cream, staying up all night, and playing Uno.

6. He was singing Lions, Tigers, and Bears, oh my!
7. Despite missing the train, we made it to 98th street by riding aggressively and skillfully on unicycles.
8. Questioning everything was the hallmark of Socrates.
9. "We began questioning the people as to where the elephant had gone, and, as usual, failed to get any definite information." George Orwell, "Shooting an Elephant"
10. "But as he went he asked, and since the road lay along crowded streets, with the vendors passing back and forth with their baskets and women going out to market, and carriages drawn by horses, and many other vehicles like the one he pulled, and everything pressing against another so that there was no possibility of running, he walked as swiftly as he was able, conscious always of the awkward bumping of his load behind him." Pearl Buck, *The Good Earth*
11. Harry has moved away from boasting about his wealth to whining about his poverty.
12. His hobbies are watching birds and cataloging them.
13. By reviewing your Latin vocabulary every other day, you will likely remember them.
14. The swimming team will be swimming at the meet on Tuesday.
15. Does my coughing bother you?

16. Did you see the new events this year—walking, climbing, and digging.
17. We made toppling the tyrant our primary goal.
18. "Locating gerunds is my specialty," said the boy with a smile.
19. Giving the new things a try is never a bad quality to possess as an exchange student in a foreign country.
20. The chairman said: "Without getting too off topic, what happened to taco Tuesday?"

ADDITIONAL EXERCISES:

1. "My child, flee from evil of every kind and from everything resembling it. Do not become angry, for anger leads to murder. Do not be jealous or quarrelsome or hot-tempered, for all these things breed murders." *Didache* 3:1-2
2. "At the Meetings Snowball often won over the majority by his brilliant speeches, but Napoleon was better at canvassing support for himself in between times. He was especially successful with the sheep. Of late the sheep had taken to bleating 'Four legs good, two legs bad' both in and out of season, and they often interrupted the Meeting with this." George Orwell, *Animal Farm*
3. "No man, for any considerable period, can wear one face to himself and another to the multitude, without finally

getting bewildered as to which may be the true." Nathaniel Hawthorne, *The Scarlet Letter*

4. Sending the letter, the soldier wondered if it would reach his worried mother who was still denying his departing to Normandy.
5. The doctor was running down the hall, wondering if his colleague gave the correct medicine to the suffering patient.
6. There were six sightings of bigfoot in the last month in midtown Manhattan.
7. He is getting fanatical about sailing around the world.

EXERCISES:

Underline the gerunds/gerund phrases and label how they are used (S, DO, IO, OP, PN, APP).

1. The warning from the headmaster was gentle but firm.
2. Hearing might leave you skeptical, but seeing will leave you believing.
3. I love swimming in that swimming pool.
4. The disease was running its course, and those who were infected improved.
5. By diligently studying every day, a child can master four languages.

6. "Above all, do not lie to yourself. A man who lies to himself and listens to his own lies comes to a point where he does not discern any truth either in himself or anywhere around him...Not respecting anyone, he ceases to love, and having no love, he gives himself up to passions and coarse pleasures, in order to occupy and amuse himself, and in his vices reaches complete bestiality, and it comes from lying continually to others and to himself." Fyodor Dostoevsky, *The Brothers Karamazov*

7. The counselor said: "Give socializing a try; you might find joy in it."

8. My traveling companion was complaining all day long, and the complaining drained me of every ounce of energy.

9. They could not prohibit her coming to the match.

10. I am not addicted to eating candy. I just love little things covered in sugar.

11. Acting is the art of keeping a large group of people from coughing. Sir Ralph Richardson

12. "He was tearing up bunches of grass, beating them against his knees to clean them and stuffing them into his mouth." George Orwell, "Shooting an Elephant"

ADDITIONAL EXERCISES:

1. Running behind a running truck is running the risk of dying.
2. My sister is excellent at breeding beta fish.
3. "Begin writing," said the teacher.
4. "The roosters had been crowing for some time, and the early pigs were already beginning their ceaseless turning of twigs and bits of wood to see whether anything to eat had been overlooked. Outside the brush house in the tuna clump, a covey of little birds chittered and flurried with their wings." John Steinbeck, *The Pearl*

20. PARTICIPLES I

20.1 Participles are verbal adjectives. As a verb, a participle can take modifiers and objects. As an adjective, a participle must modify a noun or pronoun.

- Plowing the fields, the farmer was exhausted. ("Field" is the object of "plowing," and "plowing" modifies "farmer.")
- Diligently plowing the fields, the farmer was exhausted. ("Diligently" modifies plowing, "fields" is the object of "plowing," and "plowing" modifies "farmer.")

20.2 There are two kinds of participles.

- Present participles end in -ing. For example: giving, running, and eating.
- Pay special attention to distinguish present participles from gerunds. Participles are verbal adjectives and gerunds are verbal nouns.
- Past participles use a helping word and do not end in –ing. For example: Having run the marathon, the woman was exhausted. With practice you will locate past participles with little problem.
- Past participles end in -d, -ed, -n, -en, or even -t. For example, given, run, eaten, and lent (past participle of lend).

20.3 All participles modify nouns or pronouns. To find out what a participle modifies, ask:

- Who or what is ______________________?
- Who or what was or has______________________?

If this question cannot be answered in a sensible way, there is no participle.

- The man swimming in the lake is an old classmate. Who or what is swimming? The man.
- The man having swum in the lake felt a chill down his spine. Who or what has swum? The man.
- The swimming pool is a sight to behold. Who or what is swimming? The swimming pool can't swim. So, "swimming" is an adjective.
- Astonished by the sights and sounds of the amusement park, the boy stood speechless and agape. Who or what was astonished? The boy.
- Having run its course, the Black Death took a huge toll of the population in the 14th century. Who or what has run? The Black Death.

20.4 Helpful Patterns:

- Introductory Participles. Swimming, the fish hit the tank.
- Participle before the word it modifies. Here the participle functions like an adjective. The broken mouse is next to the computer.
- Participle after the word it modifies. The man running to catch the train fell.

20.5 Participles can be tricky. The following rules will help you navigate through common pitfalls. Gerunds end in "ing," but so do many participles. The best way to tell the difference between the two is by examining the grammatical function of each word. Gerunds function as verbal nouns; participles function as verbal adjectives. Examine these sentences carefully.

- Leaving New York was a relief.
- Leaving New York, I was relieved.
- Seeing the world in my twenties was one of my main goals in life.
- Seeing the world in my twenties, I accomplished one of my main goals in life.
- I loved running the marathon.
- Hitting a ninety mile an hour pitch made the high school student feel special.
- Throwing down his glove, the batter charged the mound.

EXERCISES:

Underline the participles and draw arrows to their antecedents.

1. Following your dreams may not make you successful, but at least you are following your heart.
2. Having made a home in the cave, the castaways were relieved that they found shelter from the coming storm.
3. The famished hikers walked through the parched desert and found an oasis.

4. The unspoken law of the hallowed judge was silence in the court.
5. The monkey, picking fleas off his mate, just fell off the dangling branch.
6. His giving of money to the charity impressed many thoughtful people.
7. Racing down the street, the car careened off the road and crashed into the steel barrier.
8. The warrior threw a javelin at the man fleeing on horseback.
9. The bruised apple on the ground will invariably attract the many insects buzzing around.
10. I saw his friend walking along the road while he was whistling Vivaldi's *The Four Seasons.*
11. Why is it that so many paintings in the museum have a picture of a setting sun?
12. If that rancher catches you stealing his sheep, he will shoot first and ask questions later.
13. They have been walking for days and found no water.
14. Having been warned by the prisoner of war, the men crossed the river on a broken bridge instead of taking the paved road.
15. "Men of outstanding ability are more likely to lack the power of controlling their own people than of defeating an enemy in battle." Livy, *Ab Urbe Condita*

16. "To see him toiling up the slope inch by inch, his breath coming fast, the tips of his hoofs clawing at the ground, and his great sides matted with sweat, filled everyone with admiration." George Orwell, *Animal Farm*

17. "Aeneas' pilgrimage from Troy to Italy can be interpreted as the pilgrimage of man from spiritual goodness to spiritual betterment, as the story of man perfecting his charity in the discharge of duties toward the state and his fellow men, as the story of man gaining moral strength to perform good and avoid evil, as the story of the hardening of man into an ideal character; as the story of the problem of good and evil or, more appropriately, the struggle of good with evil." John Hiritzu, "The Identity of Aeneas"

EXAMPLE FROM LITERATURE:

Underline participles and gerunds. For participles, draw an arrow to the word it modifies. For gerunds, label how they are used.

"This great increase of the quantity of work, which, in consequence of the division of labour, the same number of people are capable of performing, is owing to three different circumstances; first, to the increase of dexterity in every particular workman; secondly, to the saving of the time which is commonly lost in passing from one species of work to another; and lastly, to the invention of a great number of machines which facilitate and abridge labour, and enable one man to do the work of many.

First, the improvement of the dexterity of the workman necessarily increases the quantity of the work he can perform, and the division of labour, by reducing every man's business to some one simple operation, and by making this operation the sole employment of his life, necessarily increased very much the dexterity of the workman. A common smith, who, though accustomed to handle the hammer, has never been used to make nails, if upon some particular occasion he is obliged to attempt it, will scarce, I am assured, be able to make above two or three hundred nails in a day, and those too very bad ones. A smith who has been accustomed to make nails, but whose sole or principal business has not been that of a nailer, can seldom with his utmost diligence make more than eight hundred or a thousand nails in a day. I have seen several boys under twenty years of age who had never exercised any other trade but that of making nails, and who, when they exerted themselves, could make, each of them, upwards of two thousand three hundred nails in a day. The making of a nail, however, is by no means one of the simplest operations. The same person blows the bellows, stirs, or mends the fire as there is occasion, heats the iron, and forges every part of the nail: In forging the head too he is obliged to change his tools. The different operations into which the making of a pin, or of a metal button, is subdivided, are all of them much more simple, and the dexterity of the person, of whose life it has been the sole business to perform them, is usually much greater. The rapidity with which some of the operations of those manufacturers are performed, exceeds what the human hand could, by those who had never seen them, be supposed capable of acquiring."

Adam Smith, *The Wealth of Nations*

Do you agree with Adam Smith that efficiency is the most important quality in an economy?

21. PARTICIPLES II

21.1 Participles can have more than one word.

- The man **having seen** the bird felt happy.

21.2 Passive participles need a helping word.

- Sisyphus exhausted himself having been forced to carry the rock. (Three words—having been forced)
- Having been demoted, the captain felt shame and regret. (Three words—having been demoted)
- Having been chastised, the boys reformed their ways. (Three words—having been chastised)
- Having been seen by the enemies in the forest, the general decided to move deeper into the forest. (Three words—having been seen)
- The sunbather fell asleep being baked by the sun. (Two words—being baked)

21.3 Progressive tenses use participles with helping verbs.

- Auxiliary verb + verb of being + participle create progressive tenses. **When this happens, consider it a *verb*.**
- Nancy was hoping for a miracle. (Progressive tense) We can make this into a simple past tense by writing the sentence: "Nancy hoped for a miracle."

- Monica will be eating Italian food for lunch and dinner. (Progressive future) We can also rewrite this sentence: "Monica will eat Italian food for lunch and dinner."
- George was swimming with the sharks at the water park. We can also rewrite this sentence: "George swam with the sharks at the water park."
- Perfect / Pluperfect / Future perfect tenses with auxiliary verb (have / had / will have) + past participle.
- Professor Hamilton has purchased three coins for the University's collection. (Has purchased = perfect tense = auxiliary verb + past participle)
- She had completed the project. (Had completed = pluperfect tense = auxiliary verb + past participle)
- The miser had saved all his money, but he tragically died before he used any of it. (Had saved = pluperfect tense = auxiliary verb + past participle)
- Luke will have married the girl of his dreams by 2030. (Will have married = future perfect tense = auxiliary verb + past participle)

21.4 The Passive voice also uses a participle. Here is the rule. Verb of being + past participle = passive voice of a verb.

- Jennifer and her friends were seen in a cab going down Madison Avenue. (Were seen = passive verb = verb of being + past participle)
- The boy was smitten with love when he saw the giant Gummy Bear. (Was smitten = passive verb = verb of being + past participle)
- She was carried on a litter through the crowd. (Was carried = passive verb = verb of being + past participle)
- The desk was scratched by a pen. (Was scratched = passive verb = verb of being + past participle)

21.5 Dangling participles:

Participles must be placed in the correct place in the sentence; otherwise, the sentence will be nonsensical. The rule of thumb is to keep the participle close to the word it modifies. Here are some examples of misplaced participles:

- Professor Grassi saw the dissertation glancing to his left. This sentence says that the dissertation is glancing.
- Picking fleas off his mate, the scientists recorded the apes.
- Foaming at the mouth, Atticus shot the rabid dog.
- Managing such a complex city, the boy respected the mayor.

EXERCISES:

Underline the participles and draw arrows to their antecedents.

1. Having walked all day, the tourists slept well.
2. "And the streets of the city shall be full of boys and girls playing in its streets." Zechariah 8:5
3. The streets of Rome, trodden by millions, still hold up well.
4. Peering out of the crack in the wall, the mouse located the cheese.
5. Having been seen by the enemies, the soldier knew to take cover behind the bushes.

6. He tossed the rotten tomato into the garbage, but she kept the bruised apple.
7. "There was once a Prince who wished to marry a Princess; but then she must be a real Princess. He travelled all over the world in hopes of finding such a lady; but there was always something wrong." Hans Christian Andersen, "The Real Princess"
8. The broken computer and the damaged mouse were on the leaning table.
9. Taking a deep breath, the swimmer dove into the pool.
10. Taking deep breaths is essential for swimmers.
11. I hate skiing.
12. The waning moon still shimmered in the night.
13. I hailed a speeding taxi for my panicking mother.
14. Rushing to do his assignment, the boy completed the wrong page in the wrong subject.
15. Children interested in music learn to develop their creative abilities.
16. Seeing the seventh game of the championship is something that I shall never forget.
17. The host of the restaurant greeted the customers with a twinkle in his eye and a spring in his step.

18. Climbing the acropolis of Athens, the boy showed determination and perseverance.

ADDITIONAL EXERCISES:

1. The guitarist's strumming moved the audience.
2. The guitarist strumming moved the audience.
3. The dour music teacher was not impressed with their playing.
4. The dour music teacher was not impressed with them playing.
5. Rushing through the exercises will harm you in the long run.
6. Rushing through the exercises, the student never learned the difference between a gerund and a participle.

EXAMPLE FROM LITERATURE:

Underline the participles and draw arrows to their antecedents.

When I was little and he was riled
It never entered my father's head
Not to flare up, roar and turn red.
Mother kept cool and smiled.

Now every night I tiptoe straight
Through my darkened kitchen for
The refrigerator door —
It opens, the inviolate!

Illumined as in dreams I take
A glass of milk, a piece of cake,
Then stealthily retire,

Mindful of how the gas-stove's black-
Browed pilot eye's blue fire
Burns into my turned back.

James Merrill, "The Midnight Snack"

MORE PARTICIPLES:

If there is a dangling participle, rewrite the sentence. If the sentence is correct, leave it alone.

1. The monkey looked intently at the girl eating a banana.

2. The bear ran after the hikers roaring.

3. The thief saw the jewels on the table peeking through the crack of the open door.

4. The lion began to crouch behind the gazelle gazing intently at his prey.

5. Fidgeting in your seat will not make the time pass any quicker.

6. Placing the jewel in his pocket, the police chased the criminal.

7. Running to hail a taxi, Dr. Jones's money fell out of his pocket.

8. Having been kneaded and pounded, the pizza chef placed his secret tomato sauce on the dough.

9. Coming out of the market, the bag of gummy bears fell on the ground.

10. I saw the dead squirrel driving down the country road.

11. My mother saw the gold Range Rover walking down the street.

12. Walking past the gravesite, an open coffin freaked me out!

13. He made a beautiful table for her with wooden legs. (This sentence does not contain a dangling participle, but there is a misplaced modifier).

14. Riding in the park on a new Brompton bicycle, a Chihuahua knocked over Mr. Gunkle.

____

____

____

15. Feeding his mate fleas, the scientist recorded the behavior of the bonobos.

____

____

____

EXAMPLE FROM LITERATURE:

Underline the participles and draw arrows to their antecedents.

"Just one month after we arrived in the U.S., Baba found a job off Washington Boulevard as an assistant at a gas station owned by an Afghan acquaintance--he'd started looking for work the same week we arrived. Six days a week, Baba pulled twelve-hour shifts pumping gas, running the register, changing oil, and washing windshields. I'd bring him lunch sometimes and find him looking for a pack of cigarettes on the shelves, a customer waiting on the other side of the oil-stained counter, Baba's face drawn and pale under the bright fluorescent lights. The electronic bell over the door would ding-dong when I walked in, and Baba would look over his shoulder, wave, and smile, his eyes watering from fatigue.

The same day he was hired, Baba and I went to our eligibility officer in San Jose, Mrs. Dobbins. She was an overweight black woman with twinkling eyes and a dimpled smile. She'd told me once that she sang in church, and I believed her—she had a voice that made me think of warm milk and honey. Baba dropped the stack of food stamps on her desk. 'Thank you but I don't want,' Baba said. 'I work always. In Afghanistan I work, in America I work. Thank you very much, Mrs. Dobbins, but I don't like it free money.'"

Khaled Hosseini, *The Kite Runner*

Try this challenging sentence pattern.

Participle	**Preposition**	**Adjective**	**Noun**
Preposition	**Adjective**	**Noun**	**Subject**
Verb	**Adjective**	**Noun**	**Noun**
Adjective	**Preposition**	**Noun**	**Participle**
Preposition	**Participle**	**Noun**	

EXAMPLE FROM LITERATURE:

Underline the participles and draw an arrow to the word it modifies; also identify gerunds and label how they are used.

"The Martians seem to have calculated their descent with amazing subtlety—their mathematical learning is evidently far in excess of ours—and to have carried out their preparations with a well-nigh perfect unanimity. Had our instruments permitted it, we might have seen the gathering trouble far back in the nineteenth century. Men like Schiaparelli watched the red planet—it is odd that for countless centuries Mars has been the star of war—but failed to interpret the fluctuating appearances of the markings they mapped so well. All that time the Martians must have been getting ready.

During the opposition of 1894 a great light was seen on the illuminated part of the disk, first at the Lick Observatory, then by Perrotin of Nice, and then by other observers. English readers heard of it first in the issue of NATURE dated August 2. I am inclined to think that this blaze may have been the casting of the huge gun, in the vast pit sunk into their planet, from which their shots were fired at us. Peculiar markings, as yet unexplained, were seen near the site of that outbreak during the next two oppositions.

The storm burst upon us six years ago now. As Mars approached opposition, Lavelle of Java set the wires of the astronomical exchange palpitating with the amazing intelligence of a huge outbreak of incandescent gas upon the planet. It had occurred towards midnight of the twelfth; and the spectroscope, to which he had at once resorted, indicated a mass of flaming gas, chiefly hydrogen, moving with an enormous velocity towards this earth. This jet of fire had become invisible about a quarter past twelve. He compared it to a colossal puff of flame suddenly and violently squirted out of the planet, 'as flaming gases rushed out of a gun.'"

H. G. Wells, *The War of the Worlds*

CLAUSE REVIEW:

Draw parentheses around subordinate clauses, drawing arrows where appropriate.

Then the angel who talked with me came forward and said to me, "Lift your eyes and see what this is that is going out." And I said, "What is it?" He said, "This is the basket that is going out." And he said, "This is their iniquity in all the land." And behold, the leaden cover was lifted, and there was a woman sitting in the basket! And he said, "This is Wickedness." And he thrust her back into the basket and thrust down the leaden weight on its opening. Then I lifted my eyes and saw, and behold, two women coming forward! The wind was in their wings. They had wings like the wings of a stork, and they lifted up the basket between earth and heaven. Then I said to the angel who talked with me, "Where are they taking the basket?" He said to me, "To the land of Shinar, to build a house for it. And when this is prepared, they will set the basket down there on its base."

Zechariah 5:5-11

What is this imagery a counterfeit of?

CLAUSES AND PARTICIPLES:

1. Draw parentheses around all dependent clauses, label whether they are adverbial or adjectival, and draw an arrow to the word they modify.
2. Underline all participles and draw arrows to their antecedents.

"Rainsford sprang up and moved quickly to the rail, mystified. He strained his eyes in the direction from which the reports had come, but it was like trying to see through a blanket. He leaped upon the rail and balanced himself there, to get greater elevation; his pipe, striking a rope, was knocked from his mouth. He lunged for it; a short, hoarse cry came from his lips as he realized he had reached too far and had lost his balance. The cry was pinched off short as the blood-warm waters of the Caribbean Sea dosed over his head.

He struggled up to the surface and tried to cry out, but the wash from the speeding yacht slapped him in the face and the salt water in his open mouth made him gag and strangle. Desperately he struck out with strong strokes after the receding lights of the yacht, but he stopped before he had swum fifty feet. A certain coolheadedness had come to him; it was not the first time he had been in a tight place. There was a chance that his cries could be heard by someone aboard the yacht, but that chance was slender and grew more slender as the yacht raced on. He wrestled himself out of his clothes and shouted with all his power. The lights of the yacht became faint and ever-vanishing fireflies; then they were blotted out entirely by the night.

Rainsford remembered the shots. They had come from the right, and doggedly he swam in that direction, swimming with slow, deliberate strokes, conserving his strength. For a seemingly endless time he fought the sea. He began to count his strokes; he could do possibly a hundred more and then—

Rainsford heard a sound. It came out of the darkness, a high screaming sound, the sound of an animal in an extremity of anguish and terror.

He did not recognize the animal that made the sound; he did not try to; with fresh vitality he swam toward the sound. He heard it again; then it was cut short by another noise, crisp, staccato. 'Pistol shot,' muttered Rainsford, swimming on.

Ten minutes of determined effort brought another sound to his ears—the most welcome he had ever heard--the muttering and growling of the sea breaking on a rocky shore. He was almost on the rocks before he saw them; on a night less calm he would have been shattered against them. With his remaining strength he dragged himself from the swirling waters. Jagged crags appeared to jut up into the opaqueness; he forced himself upward, hand over hand. Gasping, his hands raw, he reached a flat place at the top. Dense jungle came down to the very edge of the cliffs. What perils that tangle of trees and underbrush might hold for him did not concern Rainsford just then. All he knew was that he was safe from his enemy, the sea, and that utter weariness was on him. He flung himself down at the jungle edge and tumbled headlong into the deepest sleep of his life".

Richard Connell, "The Most Dangerous Game"

EXAMPLE FROM LITERATURE:

Identify the underlined words.

"There was a merchant in Bagdad who sent his servant to market **to buy provisions** and in a little while the servant came back, white and trembling, and said, Master, just now **when I was in the marketplace** I was jostled by a woman in the crowd and when I turned, I saw it was Death **that jostled me**. She looked at me and made a **threatening** gesture. Now, lend me your horse, and I will ride away from this city and avoid my fate. I will go to Samarra, and **there** Death will not find me. The merchant lent him his horse, and the servant mounted it, and he dug his spurs in its flanks and as fast as the horse could gallop, he went. Then the merchant went down **to the marketplace**, and he saw me **standing** in the crowd and he came to me and said, 'Why did you make a threating gesture to my servant **when you saw him this morning**?' 'That was not a threatening gesture,' I said, 'it was only a start of surprise. I was astonished to see him in Bagdad, for I had an appointment with him tonight in Samarra.'"

W. Somerset Maugham, "The Appointment in Samarra"

Do you believe in fate? Can you outrun it?

EXAMPLE FROM LITERATURE:

Identify the words in bold print.

"Call me Ishmael. Some years ago—never mind how long precisely—having little or no money in my purse, and nothing particular to interest me on shore, I thought I would sail about a little and see the **watery** part of the world. It is a way I have of **driving** off the spleen and **regulating** the circulation. Whenever I find myself **growing** grim about the **mouth**; whenever it is a damp, drizzly November in my soul; whenever I find myself **involuntarily pausing** before coffin warehouses, and **bringing** up the rear of every funeral I meet; and especially whenever my hypos get such an upper hand of me, that it requires a strong moral principle to prevent me from deliberately **stepping** into the street, and methodically **knocking** people's hats off—then, I account it high time to get to sea as soon as I can. This is my substitute for pistol and ball. With a philosophical flourish Cato throws himself upon his sword; I quietly take to the ship.

There is nothing surprising in this. If they but knew it, almost all men in their degree, some time or other, cherish very nearly the same **feelings** towards the ocean with me. There now is your insular city of the Manhattoes,[3] **belted** round by wharves as Indian isles by coral reefs— commerce surrounds it with her surf. Right and left, the streets take you waterward. Its extreme downtown is the battery, where that noble mole is washed by waves, and cooled by breezes, which a few hours previous were out of sight of land. Look at the crowds of water-gazers **there**. "

Herman Melville, *Moby Dick*

3 Manhattoes is a reference to people living Manhattan, the most populous city in America during Melville's day.

22. INFINITIVES I

22.1 An infinitive is composed of "to" plus the verb. It is usually used as a noun. It can also be an adjective or adverb. An infinitive is easy to identify. "To" + the "Verb" = infinitive.

- Examples: to run, to see, to eat, to be, to sing, to study, etc.

It is important to note that "to" is not a preposition. Prepositions have a noun or pronoun as an object, never a verb.

22.2 Infinitive as a noun:

- As a noun, an infinitive can function as subject, direct object, predicate nominative, and appositive.
- **To win the game** was my desire. To win = subject.
- I love **to eat**. To eat = direct object.
- My ambition in life is **to hold one world record**. To hold one world record = predicate nominative.
- John's accomplishment, **to eat ten slices of pizza**, made him famous at school (and sick). To eat ten slices of pizza = appositive.
- It would make me sick **to eat the meatloaf**. This sentence can be rewritten: "To eat the meatloaf would make me sick." To eat the meatloaf = subject.

22.3 Infinitive as an adjective:

- Like an adjective, an infinitive can be used to describe a noun.

- An adjectival infinitive always follows the noun it describes.
- This is the best pizza **to eat**. What pizza? The answer is: the best pizza to eat. You can clearly see that the infinitive is adjectival. A few more examples will make this point clear.
- This is the video **to watch** if you want to learn about carpentry.
- Whenever I take the subway, I carry a book **to read**, just in case I get caught in traffic.
- He lacked the stamina **to finish** the quest.
- Notice that all the infinitives follow the noun it modifies.

22.4 Infinitive as adverb:

- An easy way to identify an adverbial infinitive is to see if you can replace the infinitive with "in order to." If you can do this, you have an adverbial infinitive.
- She practiced the cello all night to perform well. The sentence can be rewritten: She practiced all night in order to perform well.
- We exercised to get stronger. The sentence can be rewritten: We exercised in order to get stronger.
- To win the geography competition, the boy memorized the atlas The sentence can be rewritten: In order to win the geography competition, the boy memorized the atlas.
- Notice that introductory dependent clauses need a comma.

22.5 Verbal quality of an infinitive:

- Since an infinitive has a verbal force, it can take an object.

- To win the race, the boy exercised after school. "Race" is the object of the infinitive. The infinitive "to win" is adverbial.
- I love to eat all foods. "Foods" is the object of "to eat," which is the direct object of the sentence.
- To give him an answer, I had to read three articles. What is "him" in this sentence? If you said it was an indirect object, you are correct. Infinitives can have indirect objects as well.

EXERCISES:

Underline the infinitives and identify the type of infinitive.

1. To win the war the Athenians sailed to Sicily to gain allies and resources.
2. To see her beauty is all I want.
3. I want to run for office, but my mother won't let me.
4. My goal in life is to run the triathlon and become an ironman.
5. It would give me great pleasure and a sense of accomplishment to climb K2.
6. I have a paper to write before I go to the party.
7. We have to stop right now.
8. The critics say that this is the restaurant to try.
9. She lifted weights to become stronger after her accident.

10. Mr. Putin has the ability to show towering strength and confidence no matter what is happening in his country.

11. To be able to witness his greatness is tantamount to winning the lottery.

12. The teacher asked me to carry the snacks to the recess deck.

13. To fight with bravery is what the general wanted.

14. To win the geography competition, the student studied demographic charts until midnight.

15. What did she want to accomplish by doing all that work?

16. *Braveheart* is the movie to watch if you want to see a good epic.

ADDITIONAL EXERCISES:

1. There are jewels to be found in good writing, but we will need to read for detail.

2. To buy a bouquet of flowers for his wife, John had to save his lunch money for two weeks.

3. Roy expected the boys to win the game, but he did not expect them to win by twenty points.

4. The sophomores have a paper to hand in before they go on their trip to Alaska.

5. What she wanted for Christmas was to take flying lessons.

EXERCISES:

Underline the infinitives and identify the type of infinitive and re-write them as gerunds if possible.

1. I do not like to sleep during the day.

2. She offered to bring food.

3. In order to win the speaking prize, Alberto stayed up all night and practiced his monologue.

4. My mother wanted to become a secret agent, but she married my father, who is afraid of flying.

5. To err is human.

6. The boy attempted to hide from the fierce gaze of the teacher.

7. James expected to stay in the guesthouse when he visited, but we had no room because my cousins are here for the summer.

8. Would you prefer to take the exam this week or next week?

9. The greatest game to watch would be the seventh game of the World Series in a subway series.

10. To redo the assignment was not fun, but it showed me the importance of being detailed.

11. To make friends has become difficult since moving to a new city.

23. INFINITIVES II

23.1 Complementary Infinitives:

A complementary infinitive completes the meaning of certain verbs—able, ought, dare, desire.

- He is able to do well.
- She ought to repay the money she borrowed.
- They will dare to sail the sea.
- Who desires to train for the marathon with Jessie?

Latin does the same: *possum, soleo, volo, nolo, cupio,* etc.

- *Possum arborem videre.* I am able to see a tree.

23.2 Infinitive phrases can have a "subject," but the whole phrase functions as the direct object.

- Consider the following sentence. "She asked him to carry the desk."
- The infinitive phrase consists of "him to carry the desk."
- By using the replacement method, it is clear that the infinitive phrase is the direct object. We can rewrite the sentence. "She asked it."
- Within the infinitive phrase, the word, "him" functions as the "subject," though it is in the object case, and the infinitive "to carry" functions as the verb. "The desk" is the object of the infinitive.

- Try this example. "They wanted her to be the leader."
- Use the replacement method. "They wanted it." "It" replaces "her to be the leader."
- "Her" is the subject of the infinitive phrase. Notice it is in the object case.
- The infinitive "to be" functions as the verb.
- "Leader" is a predicate nominative because of the linking verb.
- Some verbs that follow this pattern are advise, encourage, tell, order, force. Once you see the pattern, these sentences will become second nature.
- In Latin, certain verbs follow his pattern as well (*iubeo* and *cogo*).
- *Milites coegerunt viros villas relinquere.* The soldiers forced the men to leave their farmhouses.
- Indirect discourse is another example.
- *Caesar dixit milites flumen videre.* Caesar said that the soldiers saw the river.

23.3 Split infinitives:

When grammar teachers tell you not to split infinitives, they are saying that there should be no adverb between "to" and the "verb."

- To run quickly vs. to quickly run.
- To study diligently vs. to diligently study.
- To sit calmly vs. to calmly sit.
- The latter are split infinitives.

The reason why some teachers say that you should not split an infinitive is rooted in Latin. The infinitive of a Latin verb (second principal part) cannot be split.

- *Laudare, monere, cedere, audire, pungare*
- Can you split infinitives? Yes, but if it can be avoided, especially in formal writing, it is a good idea.

23.4 Some infinitives drop "to."

- She **made** me **do** the assignment again!
- When she asked me for permission, I **let** her **go**.
- The dog **can sleep** wherever he likes.

23.5 Infinitives have tense.

- To see (present)
- To have seen (perfect)
- Unlike in Latin, English does not have a future infinitive.

EXERCISES:

Underline the infinitives and identify the type.

1. She asked me to bring the cupcakes that were on the counter, but I forgot to bring them.
2. We ought to take the resources and share them with the rest of the men.
3. Shall I advise him not to invest in the company that is on the brink of bankruptcy?
4. It is commonly believed that it takes about ten years or ten thousand hours to become an expert in something.

5. We don't have to be one-dimensional.
6. Odysseus finds favor with Nausicaa, the daughter of Queen Arete and King Alcinous. She answers his questions about the island and counsels him to seek her parents who can aid him.
7. The desire to be recognized is as old as civilization.
8. "Your mother's trying to like him." writes John Ames about his wife in Marilynne Robinson's book, *Gilead*.
9. The easy path, the one of least resistance, rarely is the best one to take.
10. Without getting too deeply into this conversation, perhaps the best way forward is to consider the dead as well as the living.
11. For Clover in *Animal Farm* the spin and spell of the pigs are too strong to break.
12. Like his ancient brothers, Atlas opposes the gods. Even in his punishment, he refuses to bow or buckle.
13. As we ramp up to elections, candidates will do and say whatever it takes to gain votes.

ADDITIONAL EXERCISES:

Underline the infinitives and identify the type.

1. He was able to do what he never thought he would be able to do.

2. The propensity of humanity has always been to build cities—bigger and higher. The first act that Cain undertakes east of Eden is to build a city.

3. The rabbi asks us this week to consider something counterintuitive, not to position ourselves to gain glory but to posture ourselves to serve others.

4. "Since rats in New York live on somebody's property (yikes!), that somebody has to let rats roam free for scientists to observe." Taken from an article in *The Atlantic*.

5. When her son is old enough, she wants him to wrestle with what it means to contemplate what is less obvious, to think long and hard about beauty in a quickly moving world, and to reflect on what it means to live a good life and be a good man.

VERBAL PRACTICE:

Underline and identify all verbals and give their usage.

1. Tired, the runners cleaned up, changed their clothing, and went out to eat.

2. Nero's burning of Rome showed that he had some serious psychological and emotional issues.

3. By raising his hand in class, he was able to show that he was paying attention.

4. Placing his hand over his heart, he swore to tell the truth and nothing but the truth.

5. Riding a unicycle down the hallway, the boy adroitly jumped over a pencil and dodged a swinging door.

6. During the exam, I will be looking for clues.

7. His ambition was to master English, Sanskrit, and Latin grammar.

8. Rushing deftly to catch the train, the man was too late to make it.

9. Having been caught by the authorities, the woman promised to reform her ways.

10. Upon hearing the verdict, the sailor was saddened and went away to a deserted island.

11. "We cast a shadow on something wherever we stand, and it is no good moving from place to place to save things, because the shadow always follows. Choose a place where you won't do harm—yes, choose a place where you won't do very much harm, and stand in it for all you are worth, facing the sunshine." E. M. Forster, *A Room with a View*

12. "Can anyone be so indifferent or idle as not to care to know by what means, and under what kind of polity, almost the whole inhabited world was conquered and brought under the dominion of the single city of Rome, and that too within a period of not quite fifty-three years?" Polybius, *Histories*

MORE PRACTICE:

Underline and label each verbal or verbal phrase in the following sentences. Remember to draw arrows to words being modified.

1. Riding your bicycle in the street is a dangerous thing to do during rush hour.
2. I lifted weights to become stronger.
3. Hosting a good dinner party requires what my mother calls social skills.
4. Taking a class on speed reading was the best decision the boy made; he finished *Of Mice and Men* in 15 minutes.
5. Having discovered gold on the beach, the boy slyly placed the nuggets into his swim trunks.
6. To spill coffee on your teacher's silk dress is not the worst thing you can do, but to fail to apologize is.
7. By skimming the notes you gave me to read, I learned that cramming for exams is better than not studying.
8. Greece, sitting between two seas—the Ionian and Aegean, is proud to declare its maritime history.
9. He was baking brownies for the boys.

VERBAL AND CLAUSE PRACTICE:

Underline and label the subordinate clauses that appear in the sentences below, drawing arrows where appropriate. Label verbals.

1. When you go to Istanbul, remember to visit the Blue Mosque, which is next to Hagia Sophia.
2. If you read *Of Mice and Men*, you might shed a tear at the difficult lives of migrant workers.
3. I find that donating what I can to charity helps me to remember that I have plenty in my life.
4. To whom will you give the apple, which is on the table?
5. During a test, especially an exam, wise students will recheck their work.
6. Don't stop until you find a hidden adverbial subordinate clause in this sentence.
7. Is it true that sharks can live out of water for two days and move on land a few miles if they had to?
8. Difficulties strengthen the mind as labor does the body.
9. "Waste no more time arguing about what a good man should be. Be one." Marcus Aurelius, *Meditations*
10. "If you do not change direction, you may end up where you are heading." Lao Tzu

PUTTING IT ALL TOGETHER:

Write a sentence with the following patterns. Feel free to use any phrases that are necessary.

1. Adverbial clause – independent clause – participial phrase – participial phrase – noun clause.

2. Noun clause – independent clause – participial phrase - adverbial clause – adverbial infinitive.

EXAMPLE FROM LITERATURE:

Please identify the use and function of the underlined words, phrases, and clauses, drawing arrows when appropriate.

"In a forest of mixed growth somewhere on the eastern spurs of the Karpathians, a man stood one winter night **watching** and **listening**, as though he waited for some beast of the woods to come **within the range** of his vision, and, later, of his rifle. But the game for whose presence he kept so keen an outlook was none that figured in the sportsman's calendar as lawful and proper for the chase; Ulrich von Gradwitz patrolled the dark forest **in quest** of a human enemy.

The forest lands of Gradwitz were of wide extent and well stocked with game; the narrow strip of precipitous woodland **that lay on its outskirt** was not remarkable for the game it harboured or the shooting it afforded, but it was the most jealously guarded of all its owner's territorial possessions. A famous lawsuit, in the days of his grandfather, had wrested it from the illegal possession of a neighbouring family of petty landowners; the **dispossessed** party had never acquiesced in the judgment of the Courts, and a long series of poaching affrays and similar scandals had **embittered** the relationships between the families for three generations. The neighbour feud had grown into a personal one **since Ulrich had come to be head of his family**; if there was a man in the world **whom he detested and wished ill to** it was Georg Znaeym, the inheritor of the quarrel and the tireless game-snatcher and raider of the disputed border-forest. The feud might, perhaps, have died down or been compromised **if the personal ill-will of the two men had not stood in the way**; as boys they had thirsted for one another's blood, as men each prayed that misfortune might fall on the other, and this **wind-scourged** winter night Ulrich had banded together his foresters to watch the dark forest, not in quest of four-footed quarry, but to keep a lookout for the prowling thieves whom he suspected of being afoot from across the land boundary. The roe-buck, **which usually kept in the sheltered hollows during a storm-wind**, **were running** like driven things tonight, and there was movement and unrest among the creatures **that were wont to sleep through the dark hours**. Assuredly there was a disturbing element in the forest, and Ulrich could guess the quarter **from whence it came**."

Saki, "The Interlopers"

EXAMPLE FROM LITERATURE:

Underline all verbals, draw parentheses around subordinate clauses, and draw arrows where appropriate.

1. I was six when my mother taught me the art of invisible strength.

2. It was a strategy for winning arguments, respect from others, and eventually, though neither of us knew it at the time, chess games.

3. I learned about opening moves and why it's important to control the center early on; the shortest distance between two points is straight down the middle.

4. I learned about the middle game and why tactics between two adversaries are like clashing ideas; the one who plays better has the clearest plans for both attacking and getting out of traps.

5. By my ninth birthday, I was a national chess champion.

6. I was still some 429 points away from grand-master status, but I was touted as the Great American Hope, a child prodigy and a girl to boot.

7. Her black men advanced across the plane, slowly marching to each successive level as a single unit.

8. My white pieces screamed as they scurried and fell off the board one by one.

9. As her men drew closer to my edge, I felt myself growing lighter.

10. I rose up into the air and flew out the window.

11. Higher and higher, above the alley, over the tops of tiled roofs, where I was gathered up by the wind and pushed up toward

the night sky until everything below me disappeared and I was alone. I closed my eyes and pondered my next move.

Amy Tan, "Rules of the Game"

VERBAL TEST:

Part I

Underline and label each verbal or verbal phrase in the following sentences. Remember to draw arrows to words being modified.

1. To walk on a tightrope over tall buildings is to risk your life needlessly.
2. To become stronger and faster, I started to run in the park every morning.
3. Knowing that the Upper School loves to talk, the school therapist instituted a week of silence.
4. The boy loved his broken and bruised hymnal.
5. "Life is to be lived, not controlled, and humanity is won by continuing to play in face of certain defeat." Ralph Ellison, *Invisible Man*
6. Henry talking and chewing gum in Dr. Kim's hallowed presence will earn a trip to the office.
7. Hidden participles lurk in dark corners of sentences for devoted students of grammar to be found.

8. "Made weak by time and fate, but strong in will / To strive, to seek, to find, and not to yield." Alfred Lord Tennyson, *Ulysses.*

9. "Terror made me cruel." Emily Brontë, *Wuthering Heights*

10. "If the laws and the community of the city came to us when we were about to run away from here, or whatever it should be called, and standing over us were to ask, 'Tell me, Socrates, what are you intending to do? By attempting this deed, aren't you planning to do nothing other than destroy us, the laws, and the civic community, as much as you can? Or does it seem possible to you that any city where the verdicts reached have no force but are made powerless and corrupted by private citizens could continue to exist and not be in ruins?'" Plato, *Crito*

Part II

Draw parentheses around subordinate clauses, drawing arrows where appropriate.

1. "Not all those who wander are lost." J. R. R. Tolkien, *Fellowship of the Ring*

2. The claim, that a dollar will be equal to the Euro in value, looks doubtful.

3. When you are in town, make sure to visit the restaurant where we first met and call me.

4. Isn't it obvious by now that I will include a tricky noun clause?
5. The secret, that you will do well if you check for multiple clauses, is obvious.
6. The book I love sits on the table my mother gave me.
7. How he did what he did amazes even Dr. Long.
8. What is true today will be true tomorrow and most likely be true in the future.
9. "It isn't what you have or who you are or where you are or what you are doing that makes you happy or unhappy. It is what you think about it." Dale Carnegie, *How to Win Friends & Influence People*
10. "Real courage is when you know you're licked before you begin, but you begin anyway and see it through no matter what." Harper Lee, *To Kill a Mockingbird*

Part III

Please identify the part of speech, use, and function of the underlined words/phrases, drawing arrows where appropriate.

"It was a **matter** of chance that I should have rented a house in one of the **strangest** communities in North America. It was on that slender riotous island which extends itself due east of New York and where there are, **among** other natural curiosities, **two** unusual formations of land. Twenty miles from the city a pair of enormous eggs, identical in contour and **separated** only by a courtesy bay, **jut** out into the most **domesticated** body of saltwater in the Western Hemisphere, the great wet barnyard of Long Island Sound. They are not perfect ovals—like the egg in the Columbus story, they are both crushed flat at the contact end—but their physical resemblance must be a source of perpetual confusion to the gulls **that fly overhead**. **To the wingless** a more **arresting** phenomenon is their dissimilarity in every particular **except** shape and size.

I lived at West Egg, the—well, the less fashionable of the two, **though** this is a most superficial tag **to express** the bizarre and not a little sinister contrast between them. My house was at the **very** tip of the egg, only fifty yards from the Sound, and squeezed between two huge places that rented for twelve or fifteen thousand a season. The one on my right was a colossal affair by any standard—it was a factual imitation of some Hôtel de Ville in Normandy, with a tower on one side, **spanking** new under a thin beard of raw ivy, and a marble **swimming** pool and more than forty acres of lawn and garden. It was Gatsby's **mansion**."

Scott Fitzgerald, *The Great Gatsby*

Part IV—Write Your Own Sentences.

1. Write a sentence with the following features:
    - A noun clause direct object
    - A participle
    - A subordinating conjunction

____

Write a sentence with the following features:

- An adverbial prep phrase at the end of the sentence
- An infinitive
- A gerund phrase as a subject

Write a sentence with the following features:

- A gerund subject used within a noun clause DO
- The word "whom" used correctly
- Present participle

Congratulations for reaching the end of the book. You have learned the foundations of English grammar from nouns and verbs to various uses of the infinitive. You are now able to break down any sentence, which means you are in a better position to appreciate the artistry of authors and write your own prose with greater awareness and skill. Come back to this book from time to time as a reference. And when you have the energy, move onto Book 3, where you will learn about punctuation, common errors, and stylistic considerations.

THE END!

ABOUT THE AUTHOR

John Lee is an educator who seeks to inspire students to achieve excellence in their studies and their lives. He has taught at St. Thomas Choir School, Drew University, Nyack College, St. Bernard's School, and The Geneva School of Manhattan. He obtained his M.A., M.Phil. and Ph.D. in history from Yale University. His essays have appeared in *The Banner, Mere Orthodoxy, Christianity Today,* and a number of other outlets. He lives in New York City and East Hampton with his wife and two children.